CATHOLIC SOCIAL
TEACHING

CATHOLIC SOCIAL TEACHING

Our Best Kept Secret

Peter J. Henriot
Edward P. DeBerri
Michael J. Schultheis

 ORBIS BOOKS
Maryknoll, New York

 DOVE COMMUNICATIONS
Melbourne, Australia

CENTER OF CONCERN
Washington D.C. 20017

Third Printing, February 1990

First U.S. edition of *Our Best Kept Secret: The Rich Heritage of Catholic Social Teaching* © 1985 by the Center of Concern, Washington, DC 20017.

Revised and enlarged edition of *Our Best Kept Secret* © 1987 by the Center of Concern.

The present book is a revised and enlarged edition of the 1987 version of *Our Best Kept Secret*. The present work © 1988 by Orbis Books, Maryknoll, NY 10545, and the Center of Concern, 3700 13th St., N.E., Washington, DC 20017.

Published in Australia by Collins Dove, P.O. Box 316, Blackburn, Victoria 3130.

ORBIS/ISBN 0-88344-632-4

COLLINS DOVE/ISBN 0 85924 7201

**We fondly dedicate this book to our colleague,
Philip Land, S.J.**

*For many years he has been
a major force in the formulation
of the Church's social teaching,
a clear teacher of its message,
and a strong personal witness
of its call to peace and justice*

CONTENTS

PREFACE

At the close of the Second Vatican Council in 1965, the Catholic Church was reminded in a powerful fashion of its contemporary mission in the world today. In the opening lines of *The Church in the Modern World (Gaudium et Spes)* the Council stated:

> The joys and hopes, the sorrows and anxieties, of the women and men of this age, especially those who are poor or in any way oppressed, these are the joys and hopes, the sorrows and anxieties, of the followers of Jesus Christ.

Just what it means to take up the "joys and hopes, sorrows and anxieties" of our sisters and brothers today is the task spelled out in the Church's social teaching. This body of principles, guidelines, and applications has developed in a rich fashion especially during the past one hundred years. It now provides a compelling challenge for responsible Christian living today.

In order to make more widely known this social teaching of the Church, the Center of Concern several years ago prepared a small "primer" to introduce the background and key lessons of the teaching. The immediate and widespread popularity of *Our Best Kept Secret* encouraged us to revise and enlarge the original version twice. *Catholic Social Teaching* is the fourth version of the work. It adds treatment of the latest social encyclical of Pope John Paul II, *The Social Concerns of the Church (Sollicitudo Rei Socialis*, 1988), as well as the three major pastoral letters of the United States Bishops, on peace, economic justice, and mission. It also includes four significant Third World documents, two from Latin America, and one each from Africa and Asia.

The introductory material has been expanded to include comment on the new documents, and an outline of each of those documents is presented in Part Two. Paragraph number citations make the use of the detailed outlines even more helpful, facilitating reference to the original documents. The annotated bibliography has been updated.

The original version of *Our Best Kept Secret* was prepared for use by the Church in Africa and has been reprinted several times there. The subsequent U.S. version (published in 1985) circulated eight thousand copies. This was reprinted in the Philippines for Asian circulation. The second U.S. edition (1987) has circulated ten thousand copies. It has been translated into Spanish in Argentina, and published in an adapted version in Great Britain.

The authors express deep gratitude to the following for their assistance in earlier versions of this book: Phil Land, S.J., Simon Smith, S.J., Anne Hope, Maurice Monette, O.M.I., Ruth Coyne, Cindy Fowler, and David Simmons. Lucien Chauvin helped greatly in the production of the present edition.

The Center of Concern is pleased to collaborate with Orbis Books in publication of *Catholic Social Teaching: Our Best Kept Secret*. We are grateful for a grant from the Catholic Social Thought Project of the University of San Francisco, which made possible the 1987 version.

In November 1986, the U.S. Catholic Bishops released the final version of their major pastoral letter entitled *Economic Justice for All: Catholic Social Teaching and the U.S. Economy*. The Bishops expressly call for "renewed emphasis" on Catholic social teaching in all our educational institutions, and express their hope that "through our continual reflection . . . we will be able to help refine Catholic social teaching and contribute to its further development" (#360).

It is the sincere prayer of the Center of Concern that *Catholic Social Teaching: Our Best Kept Secret* will continue to assist the Christian community, in the United States and elsewhere, to engage more effectively in the linking of faith and justice through an increased knowledge of, appreciation for, and response to the rich heritage of Catholic social teaching.

Peter J. Henriot, S.J.
Center of Concern
Washington, D.C.
April 11, 1988
25th Anniversary of *Peace on Earth*

PART ONE

HISTORICAL BACKGROUND

1

OUR BEST KEPT SECRET

"The best kept secret in the Roman Catholic Church in the United States!" That is how the Church's social teaching has frequently been described. *That* the church has a developed body of teaching on social, economic, political, and cultural matters and *what* that body says seem to have been forgotten—or were never known—by a majority of the Roman Catholic community in the United States.

At least it would seem that all too few Catholics know about the Church's social teaching if we are to judge from the reactions of many U.S. Catholics to their Bishops' Peace Pastoral of 1983 and Economics Pastoral of 1986. These two important letters of the National Conference of Catholic Bishops (NCCB) have been called "radical" and criticized for not being authentically Catholic. Yet both draw heavily for their inspiration and direction upon the documents authored in recent decades by Popes, the Second Vatican Council, the Synods of Bishops, and national conferences of Bishops.

The traditional roots of the U.S. Bishops' messages can be readily noted:

The Challenge of Peace: God's Promise and Our Response examines the morality of war and peace and questions the arms race from the perspectives presented by Pope John XXIII in his encyclical *Peace on Earth* (1963), and by the statement *The Church in the Modern World* (1963) of Vatican II.

Economic Justice for All: Catholic Social Teaching and the U.S. Economy addresses such issues as unemployment, international trade, welfare policy, and governmental planning with perspectives raised in Pope Paul VI's *Progress of People* (1967), the Synod of Bishops' *Justice in the World* (1971), and Pope John Paul II's *On Human Labor* (1981).

Not to know the foundation and background of these pastoral letters is to be seriously hampered in understanding their message and responding to their call.

In the not too distant past, courses in the social encyclicals were routinely offered in colleges and seminaries. Many adult education programs—such as labor schools—provided intense study of their teachings and applications. Popular handbooks explained the significance of the messages to a wide audience. But this has not been the case in recent years. Today, it is a rare theology department or seminary which provides a course dealing specifically with the Church's social teaching. The ordinary Catholic probably has heard very few homilies in her or his local parish on the topic of the social teachings.

Why is this so? Why are we keeping the social teachings "secret"? Many factors seem to have contributed to this unfortunate situation.

1. The documents usually seem to be rather abstract, dry in content, and not very attractive to pick up and read.
2. The topics frequently are quite challenging, dealing as they do with controversial social issues, and therefore they may disturb readers and make them uncomfortable.
3. A "papal encyclical" is, at least in many people's minds, almost immediately associated with *On Human Life (Humanae Vitae,* 1968) and all the debates, disputes, and dissent over the Church's position on birth control.
4. In general, authoritative statements—whether from Church or government—have less attraction today than acts of authentic witness.

But it is noteworthy that recently there has been a small resurgence of interest in the social teachings. The topic of what the

Church has to say on the political and economic issues of the day is gaining new attention in ever wider circles. It is true that this leads to many lively political debates. But it also reveals a much deeper longing on the part of Catholics and others, in response to the needs of the day.

The serious crises we face in the social order, nationally and internationally, have challenged Catholics as parents, citizens, teachers, workers, business and professional people, politicians, etc. We are looking around for explanations and guidelines which give us a Christian perspective on the contemporary social events and issues confronting our nation. What can we say, as Christians, about peace and the arms race, economic justice, international development, racism and sexism, human rights, the dignity of all persons and the sacredness of human life, work and labor unions, etc.?

More and more people are rediscovering—or discovering for the first time—the rich heritage of the Church's social teachings. We are responding with enthusiasm and sometimes with astonishment: "I didn't know there were so many good things in the encyclicals!"

Easy answers to hard problems cannot be found in the social teachings. We must resist the temptation to look for clear solutions. But what can be found is a *social wisdom* based on:

—biblical insights
—the tradition of the early writers of the Church
—scholastic philosophy
—theological reflection
—and the contemporary experience of the People of God struggling to live out faith in justice.

What we offer in this small book is by no means a thorough presentation of the Church's social teaching as it is relevant to the United States. Rather, by way simply of an *introduction*, we aim to:

1. Provide an overview of historical development of the teaching.
2. Note the major thrust of the teaching as it has been applied to the issues of the day.

3. Show its use in documents of the Church in the United States and in the Third World.
4. Stimulate further study and reflection.

The *summaries* of the documents are intended to open up the principal elements of the teaching in an easy-to-grasp outline form. Readers are encouraged to use these summaries in conjunction with the full text of the documents themselves and to relate the documents to their historical contexts. This is essential if one is to appreciate the ongoing and dynamic relationship of the Church to a complex and changing world.

It is obvious, of course, that "introductions" and "summaries" are no substitute for actually reading, studying, and praying over the texts themselves. Then applications must be made to the real life situations of social, economic, political, and cultural conditions in the United States and around the world. This is the way to make the faith message of these documents come alive in the institutions and values of our day.

The aim of this book is *commitment*. Commitment to a faith that does justice. For since the Second Vatican Council we in the Church have come to understand more fully and appreciate more deeply that a "living faith" leads directly to a "loving action" in the transformation of the world.

2

An Evolving Social Message

FROM POPE LEO XIII TO THE SECOND VATICAN COUNCIL

Reconstructing the Social Order

The Church's social teaching in the modern period dates from 1891, when Pope Leo XIII in the encyclical letter, *The Condition of Labor (Rerum Novarum)*, spoke out against the inhuman conditions which were the normal plight of working people in industrial societies. He recognized that the three key factors underlying economic life are workers, productive property, and the state. He also indicated that their just and equitable interrelationship is the crucial issue of Catholic social teaching. Because of the principles which he set forth to guide in the formation of a just society, this document has become known as the *Magna Carta* for a humane economic and social order.

In 1931, on the occasion of the fortieth anniversary of *The Condition of Labor*, Pope Pius XI composed the next major social encyclical, *The Reconstruction of the Social Order (Quadragesimo Anno)*. Writing in the midst of a severe, world-wide economic depression, Pius XI addressed the issue of social injustice and called for the reconstruction of the social order along the lines originally set forth by Leo XIII. He reaffirmed the right and the duty of the Church to address social issues.

While condemning capitalism and unregulated competition, Pius XI also condemned communism for its promotion of class struggle and the narrow reliance for leadership on the working class (the so-called "dictatorship of the proletariat"). He stressed the social responsibilities of private property and the rights of working people to a job, to a just wage, and to organize to claim their rights. He also pointed out the positive role of governments in promoting the economic good of all people in society. Economic undertakings should be governed by justice and charity as the principal laws of social life.

During World War II, Pope Pius XII delivered several important "Christmas Messages" in which he outlined the just international order necessary for global peace. He encouraged the cooperation which resulted in the institution of the United Nations. His vision accounts for the long-standing commitment of strong support given to the United Nations by the Church's social teaching.

Thirty years after Pius XI's great letter, Pope John XXIII wrote two major social encyclical letters on the central issues of his day. In *Christianity and Social Progress (Mater et Magistra*, 1961) and *Peace on Earth (Pacem in Terris*, 1963), Pope John set forth a number of principles to guide both Christians and policy makers in addressing the gap between rich and poor nations and the threats to world peace. He called on committed Christians and "all people of good will" to work together to create local, national, and global institutions which would both respect human dignity and promote justice and peace. He emphasized that the growing interdependence among nations in a world community called for an effective world government which would look to the rights of the individual human person and promote the universal common good.

A major contribution of John XXIII was his emphasis in *Peace on Earth* on social and economic rights and not just on legal and political rights. Among the economic rights were the right to work and the right to a just wage. Reflecting the development of the United Nations' *Universal Declaration of Human Rights* (1948), this promotion of economic rights finds strong reaffirmation in the U.S. Bishops' Economics Pastoral.

The Coming of a "World" Church

When Pope John XXIII convened the Second Vatican Council in October 1962, he opened the windows of the Church to the fresh air of the modern world. This Twenty-First Ecumenical Council was the first to reflect a truly world church. For three years Cardinals and Bishops from every continent and from nearly every nation on the globe assembled to discuss the nature of the Church and its mission to and in the world.

The Council leaders were acutely sensitive to the problems of a world polarized by ideologies and threatened by nuclear warfare. They witnessed at first hand the effects of a spiraling arms race, environmental destruction, and the growing disparity between rich and poor. They also recognized that the Church, by virtue of the mission which Christ had entrusted to it, has a unique responsibility for shaping values and institutions in that world.

In many respects, Vatican II represented the end of one era and the beginning of a new era. The enthusiasm and energies of the Age of Enlightenment had been spent. This philosophical movement of the eighteenth century, marked by a rejection of traditional social, religious, and political ideas and an emphasis on rationalism, had culminated in the holocaust in Europe and in a world sharply divided. These events had dashed hopes that secular society, based on human reason severed from religious faith, would lead to unending progress. Instead a misguided rationalism had unleashed forces which threatened to destroy the world.

The Church had turned inward in reaction to a rationalistic age which demeaned religious belief. Religion, more and more defined as a "private" affair between the individual and God, was relegated to a marginal role in secular society. At the same time, the Church channeled its energies outwardly to evangelize the "mission lands" of Africa, Asia, and Latin America.

During Vatican II, the Council leaders rejected that marginal role in society as inconsistent with the unique religious mission which Christ had given to his Church. They disclaimed for the Church any unique and proper mission in the political, economic, or social order. But in *The Church in the Modern World (Gaudium et Spes,* 1965), they affirmed that the specifically religious mission of the Church did give it "a function, a light, and an energy which can serve to structure and consolidate the human community according to the divine law. As a matter of fact, when circumstances of time and place create the need, it can and indeed should initiate activities on behalf of all people" (#42).

Yet the Council, in relating the Church to the wider society, did caution against any disrespect shown toward other views which were religiously founded. This was the message of the great statement *On Religious Freedom* (*Dignitatis Humanae*, 1965), a statement strongly influenced by the experience of the Church in the United States.

THE CHURCH AFTER THE SECOND VATICAN COUNCIL

The Faith That Does Justice

Since Vatican II, statements by Pope Paul VI and Pope John Paul II, by Synods of Bishops, and by regional and national conferences of Bishops have helped to clarify the role of the Church in meeting its new responsibilities in a rapidly changing world. The Popes and the Bishops have been acutely aware that the search for God's word in the events of history is not a simple task. They also have recognized that the Church has neither immediate nor universally valid solutions to all the complex and pressing problems of society.

Three documents in particular have contributed to the Church's present understanding of its new responsibilities. Pope Paul VI's encyclical letter *The Development of Peoples* (*Populorum Progressio*, 1967) responded to the cries of the world's poor and hungry and addressed the structural dimensions of global injustice. Speaking of the right of all to integral human development, he appealed to both rich and poor nations to work together in a spirit of solidarity to establish an order of justice and bring about the renewal of the temporal order. To encourage this noble enterprise he set up a Pontifical Commission on Justice and Peace.

The second document was the apostolic letter *A Call to Action* (*Octogesima Adveniens*, 1971), which Paul VI wrote on the occasion of the eightieth anniversary of *The Condition of Labor*. Here Paul VI acknowledged the difficulties inherent in establishing a just social order and pointed to the role of local Christian communities in meeting this responsibility.

It is up to the Christian communities to analyze with objectivity the situation which is proper to their own country, to shed on it the light of the Gospel's unalterable words and to draw principles of reflection, norms of judgment and directives for action from the social teaching of the Church (#4).

In effect Paul VI insisted that God calls Christians and communities to be both *hearers* and *doers* of the word. Christians who are faithful to the Gospel will be engaged in an ongoing "incarnational" process which involves three separate moments:

1. Evaluation and analysis of their contemporary situation.
2. Prayer, discernment, and reflection, bringing the light of the Gospel and the teachings of the Church to bear on the situation.
3. Pastoral action which fights injustices and works for the transformation of society, thus laboring to make the "reign" of God a reality.

Also in 1971, representatives of the world's Bishops gathered in a Synod in Rome and prepared the statement *Justice in the World*. In this third document, which illustrates the influence of a truly world Church, the Bishops identified the dynamism of the Gospel with the hopes of people for a better world. In what has become a well-known and frequently cited statement, they asserted:

Action on behalf of justice and participation in the transformation of the world fully appear to us as a constitutive dimension of the preaching of the Gospel, or in other words, of the Church's mission for the redemption of the human race and its liberation from every oppressive situation (#6).

This vision of the social mission of the Church, of a Church that "does" justice as an integral element of its faith, is slowly leavening the universal Church. It is manifest in the activities and teachings of regional and national conferences of Bishops, such as those of the U.S. Church and of the Latin American Church in Medellín (1968) and Puebla (1979). It is being proclaimed in the faith and actions of countless individuals, communities, and local churches throughout the world. Central to this vision, the Synod noted, is that the Church which would proclaim justice to the world must itself be seen to be just.

Evangelization and Justice

Pope Paul VI advanced the social teaching of the Church further in his *Evangelization in the Modern World (Evangelii Nuntiandi*, 1975). Here he emphasized that preaching the Gospel would be incomplete if it did not take into account human rights and the themes of family life, life in society, peace, justice, and development. Liberation—in both its spiritual and its temporal senses—must be proclaimed. The plan of the Redemption includes combating injustice.

This strong link between the Gospel and social justice has been emphasized repeatedly by Pope John Paul II. In his first encyclical letter, *Redeemer of Humankind (Redemptor Hominis*, 1979), he stated that when we put the human at the center then we see contemporary society in need of redemption. John Paul II challenged disrespect of the environment and an uncritical stance toward technological advance. *Rich in Mercy (Dives Misericordiae*, 1980) presented mercy as social love, demonstrating its close link to justice.

John Paul II's next important social teaching came in *On Human Work (Laborem Exercens*, 1981). "The priority of labor over capital" was enunciated as central to the just society. The Pope criticized an "economism" which would reduce humans to mere instruments of production. He called the workers' struggle for justice the dynamic element in contemporary society, emphasizing the need for greater "solidarity" around the world. *On Human Work* also takes up again a common theme in the Church's social teaching, the critique of liberal capitalism and the warning against collectivist socialism.

Application of this emphasis on the linkage between evangelization and justice has been effectively made by the Latin American bishops. In Medellín (1968) they presented Jesus as liberator from sin in both personal and social dimensions, and showed the consequences for the Church of a mission which promotes peace and justice. The Puebla documents (1979) developed further the mission of evangelization and stressed the role of base communities and the laity. Evangelization and liberation were seen as integral.

Other examples of a Third World connection between the Christian vision and the reality of today's challenges are found in the 1981 statement of the Bishops of the African continent and the 1974 statement of the Bishops of Asia. The African statement presented a pastoral program for the local churches which included a strong emphasis on education for justice. At the national level, the need to speak out for justice was stressed; at the international level, an appeal was made for more just structures. In the Asian statement, the Bishops emphasized that evangelization requires a dialogue with the poor and that this dialogue must include a focus on the situations of injustice and oppression.

Further development in the social teaching of the Church can be found in two recent statements by Cardinal Joseph Ratzinger of the Congregation for the Defense of the Faith. *Instruction on Certain Aspects of the Theology of Liberation* (1984) and *Instruction on Christian Freedom and Liberation* (1986) both were released with the explicit approval of their contents by John Paul II. These statements can be seen as cautions against some strains of liberation theology—not, it should be noted in honesty, the main streams. But even more important, the Ratzinger documents reiterated the more recent emphasis of Catholic social teaching on the need for structural transformation in order to achieve social justice, on the centrality of the liberation theme itself in the biblical message and hence the entire Christian message, and on the preferential option for the poor.

Peace, Justice, and Politics

The United States Catholic Church has taken seriously Paul VI's call to apply the social teachings to "the situation which is proper to their own country." A series of statements have come from the National Conference of Catholic Bishops (NCCB) and its policy arm, the United States Catholic Conference (USCC). The three most important statements form a "trilogy" of pastoral letters, on the topics of peace (1983), economic justice (1986), and mission (1986). Basic to each pastoral letter is its foundation in the tradition of the social teaching enunciated by the Popes and Vatican II.

The arms race and international tensions were addressed in *The Challenge of Peace: God's Promise and Our Response* (1983). The pastoral letter came twenty years after John XXIII's *Peace on Earth* and reiterated strongly the need to build the structures of peace. It stirred considerable controversy by reason of its challenge to the Reagan administration's defense policy, including its moral analysis of the stance of nuclear deterrence. While relying primarily on the tradition of the just war theory, the letter also emphasized the importance of the non-violent (pacifist) tradition. One consequence of the letter was that moral considerations have entered more widely into the politics of public debate over military defense policies.

The social justice aspects of topics such as unemployment, poverty, agriculture, and global interdependence were treated in *Economic Justice for All: Catholic Social Teaching and the U.S. Economy* (1986). As they moved into making specific policy recommendations, the U.S. Bishops repeated a significant distinction they had earlier made in the Peace Pastoral by acknowledging that their judgments and recommendations "do not carry the same moral authority as our statements of universal moral principles and formal church teaching" (#135). Their prudential judgments on specific economic issues have direct political consequences: they will, and are designed to, stimulate debate and dialogue. Central to the Economics Pastoral, rooted in its scriptural foundation, was the emphasis on the option for the poor.

The option for the poor came up again in *To the Ends of the Earth* (1986), when the U.S. Bishops spoke of a holistic approach to mission, one which necessarily includes liberation. A new self-understanding of the Church was stressed in this pastoral letter, with Church being essentially identified with mission in the widest sense. It is a significant commentary on the "seamless garment" character of Catholic social teaching that the Mission Pastoral said that the concern for mission springs from the sense of discipleship which has been articulated in the pastoral letters on peace and on economic justice.

The latest encyclical of Pope John Paul II, *The Social Concerns of the Church* (*Sollicitudo Rei Socialis*, 1988), pushed the link between peace and justice further by emphasizing the plight of Third World development in terms of the harmful influence of superpower confrontation. Commemorating *The Development of Peoples*, John Paul II asserted that little or no development actually had occurred since Paul VI's strong call in 1968. He strongly criticized the desire for profit and the thirst for power, calling them "structures of sin." The Pope offered a solution in the direction of a politics of solidarity.

3

A SHIFTING SOCIAL APPROACH

The body of Catholic social teaching is by no means a fixed set of tightly developed doctrine. Rather, it is a collection of key themes which has evolved in response to the challenges of the day. Rooted in biblical orientations and reflections on Christian tradition, the social teaching shows a lively evolution marked by shifts both in *attitude* and *methodology*. What informs the teaching of John Paul II today differs from what informed the teaching of Leo XIII almost a century ago—even though both ground their message in the same faith in the God revealed by and in Jesus Christ. This means that the approach taken in the Church's social teaching has been undergoing some significant shifting that we should pay attention to in order to appreciate its contemporary relevance.

SHIFTS IN ATTITUDE

The Second Vatican Council marked a new period in the life of the Church. One fundamental aspect of this new period was a change in the Church's attitude toward the world. Such a change has had profound consequences for the themes and emphases of the Church's social teaching. Philip Land, S.J., of the Center of Concern, has identified four distinct aspects in this change in attitude (see "Catholic Social Teaching: 1891–1981," *Center Focus*, no. 43, May 1981).

1. An assault on political apathy. Many church leaders, theologians, and loyal critics continue to ask how it was possible for the Church to be largely silent and passive in the face of the atrocities of the Second World War. The answer at least in part is that the Church and religion had become confined to the private arena. Rejecting this privatization and the political apathy it engenders, Vatican II recognized that the Church shares responsibility for secular as well as for religious history. Pope Paul VI insisted in *A Call to Action* that politics is a "vocation" aimed at the transformation of society.

2. A commitment to the "humanization" of life. The Council emphasized the Church's responsibility for the world, a world which God created and Jesus walked upon. Moreover, as the Council leaders affirmed and as Pope John Paul II stated in *On Human Work*, people can rightly consider that they are continuing the Creator's work through their own labor and contributing to the realization in history of the divine plan. From these attitudes a respect develops for the rightful autonomy of the secular world.

3. A commitment to world justice. The Bishops in their 1971 Synod statement, *Justice in the World*, urged that justice be sought at all levels of society but especially between rich and powerful nations and those that are poor and weak. The Bishops declared that the doing of justice is a "constitutive dimension of the preaching of the Gospel" (#6). A truly global vision is the hallmark of the Christian.

4. Preferential option for the poor. The Church has always understood that Christ identifies with the poor and underprivileged. But it now looks at this truth with new urgency and new pastoral consequences. In reading the "signs of the times," Christians see God's face above all in the faces of suffering and wounded people. Consequently, fidelity to Christ requires an identification with and an "option" for the poor. In the last few years this conviction has become a priority for the Church in its theological reflection and pastoral action. Originally an insight of the Latin American Church, the option for the poor has been assumed by the universal Church in the statements of John Paul II. It has had a strong influence on the U.S. Bishops' Economics Pastoral.

SHIFTS IN METHODOLOGY

Several methodological changes have accompanied the attitudinal changes noted above. Land identifies five significant shifts in the methodology of the Church's social teaching.

1. Imaging the Church as the "People of God." Vatican II, in *The Nature of the Church (Lumen Gentium*, 1964), emphasized the Church as "People of God." This biblical image holds important implications not only for ecclesiology, but also for the Church's approach to the social order. The Church as "People of God" lifts the faithful from a passive role to an active role in defining and shaping their history in the contemporary world. But the Church does not claim any special, unique competence in technical questions. It does not possess all the answers, but searches for them in cooperation with others. As Paul VI indicated in *A Call to Action*, it is up to local Christian communities to join others of good will in seeking solutions to pressing social questions (#4).

2. Reading the "signs of the times." It is a basic Christian belief that God continues to speak in and through human history. This truth was reaffirmed by Vatican II. Consequently, the Church has "the duty of scrutinizing the signs of the times and of interpreting them in the light of the gospel" (*The Church in the Modern World*, #4). This statement in effect introduced a new method of "doing" theology.

The Church looks to the world and discovers there God's presence. Signs both reveal God's presence in the world and manifest God's designs for the world. Implicit in this truth is that theology must go beyond the purely deductive and speculative. History ceases to be the mere context for the application of binding principles, which are derived uniquely from speculative and philosophical reasoning. It becomes the place of on-going revelation.

3. The movement away from a narrow adherence to natural law. As the social teaching has shifted from the deductive to the inductive and the historical, there has been a movement away from a rigidly interpreted natural law ethic. The defined absolutes of an earlier natural law have been replaced by the search for the objectively true, which is seen to be the objectively human insofar as that can be disclosed.

This search for the objectively human is rooted in experience and embraces an holistic approach to human decision making. External truths, insofar as these can be possessed, need to be filtered through personal experiences, observation, memory, and general societal history. This process of human decision making necessarily involves the struggle to understand the full human reality and to discover the call of God in the midst of that reality.

4. The primacy of love. Reason was the primary shaper of the Church's earlier formulation of social teaching. In recent decades, however, the social teaching has been increasingly shaped by the primacy of love. The primacy of love has three meanings in this context. First, love is at the heart of the virtue of justice and brings the actions of justice to their fullest potential, meaning, and life. Second, love is the motivation to act on behalf of justice. Third, the fundamental option of love, which the heart makes for God as the ground of our being, produces moral action. Reason is not discarded in the social teachings, but put in its proper place.

5. An orientation to pastoral planning and action. The evolving methodology of the Church's social teaching is also praxis-oriented. Praxis, the action that comes out of reflection and leads back to reflection, can be viewed as the end result of an option which one makes in the struggle for justice. The corollary is that correct action ("orthopraxis") completes correct doctrine ("orthodoxy").

The earlier methodology of Catholic social teaching often led to social idealism. It isolated reason from a relationship of dialogue with experience, commitment, and action. But from the praxis side, the starting point of pastoral and social reflection is people in their struggle, in their needs, and in their hopes. Praxis thus becomes a true force for understanding and developing all authentic social teaching.

4

TWELVE MAJOR LESSONS

Any list of "major lessons" of Catholic social teaching is difficult to draw up (there is such a large body of church teaching) and dangerous to publish (what about all the important items left out?). Offered with all due caution, therefore, is the following list of key emphases which characterize Catholic social teaching today. The documents suggested in parentheses illustrate the major lesson particularly well.

1. Link of religious and social dimensions of life. The "social"—the human construction of the world—is not "secular" in the sense of being outside of God's plan, but is intimately involved with the dynamic of the Reign of God. Therefore faith and justice are necessarily linked together (*The Church in the Modern World*).

2. Dignity of the human person. Made in the image of God, women and men have a preeminent place in the social order. Human dignity can be recognized and protected only in community with others. The fundamental question to ask about social development is: What is happening to people? (*Peace on Earth*).

3. Political and economic rights. All human persons enjoy inalienable rights, which are political-legal (e.g., voting, free speech, migration) and social-economic (e.g., food, shelter, work, education). These are realized in community. Essential for the promotion of justice and solidarity, these rights are to be respected and protected by all the institutions of society (*Peace on Earth*).

4. Option for the poor. A preferential love should be shown to the poor, whose needs and rights are given special attention in God's eyes. "Poor" is understood to refer to the economically disadvantaged who, as a consequence of their status, suffer oppression and powerlessness (*Call to Action*).

5. Link of love and justice. Love of neighbor is an absolute demand for justice, because charity must manifest itself in actions and structures which respect human dignity, protect human rights, and facilitate human development. To promote justice is to transform structures which block love (*Justice in the World*).

6. Promotion of the common good. The common good is the sum total of all those conditions of social living—economic, political, cultural—which make it possible for women and men readily and fully to achieve the perfection of their humanity. Individual rights are always experienced within the context of promotion of the common good. There is also an international common good (*Christianity and Social Progress*).

7. Subsidiarity. Responsibilities and decisions should be attended to as close as possible to the level of individual initiative in local communities and institutions. Mediating structures of families, neighborhoods, community groups, small businesses, and local governments should be fostered and participated in. But larger government structures do have a role when greater social coordination and regulation are necessary for the common good (*The Reconstruction of the Social Order*).

8. Political participation. Democratic participation in decision making is the best way to respect the dignity and liberty of people. The government is the instrument by which people cooperate together in order to achieve the common good. The international common good requires participation in international organizations (Pius XII, "Christmas Message," 1944).

9. Economic justice. The economy is for the people and the resources of the earth are to be shared equitably by all. Human work is the key to contemporary social questions. Labor takes precedence over both capital and technology in the production process. Just wages and the right of workers to organize are to be respected (*On Human Work*).

10. Stewardship. All property has a "social mortgage." People are to respect and share the resources of the earth, since we are all part of the community of creation. By our work we are co-creators in the continuing development of the earth (*On Human Work*).

11. Global solidarity. We belong to one human family and as such have mutual obligations to promote the rights and development of all people across the world, irrespective of national boundaries. In particular, the rich nations have responsibilities toward the poor nations, and the structures of the international order must reflect justice (*The Development of Peoples; The Social Concerns of the Church*).

12. Promotion of peace. Peace is the fruit of justice and is dependent upon right order among humans and among nations. The arms race must cease and progressive disarmament take place if the future is to be secure. In order to promote peace and the conditions of peace, an effective international authority is necessary (*Peace on Earth*).

PART TWO

DOCUMENT

OUTLINES

INTRODUCTION TO SUMMARIES

These outlines constitute an attempt to summarize some of the major documents of the Catholic Church's modern social tradition. They are designed to highlight the key points of each document and serve as a reference for further study and explanation. They are not a substitute for a thorough reading of each document.

The following documents are outlined in this book:

1. *The Condition of Labor (Rerum Novarum)*. Encyclical Letter of Pope Leo XIII, 1891.

2. *The Reconstruction of the Social Order (Quadragesimo Anno)*. Encyclical Letter of Pope Pius XI, 1931.

3. *Christianity and Social Progress (Mater et Magistra)*. Encyclical Letter of Pope John XXIII, 1961.

4. *Peace on Earth (Pacem in Terris)*. Encyclical Letter of Pope John XXIII, 1963.

5. *The Church in the Modern World (Gaudium et Spes)*. Second Vatican Council, 1965.

6. *The Development of Peoples (Populorum Progressio)*. Encyclical Letter of Pope Paul VI, 1967.

7. *A Call to Action (Octogesima Adveniens)*. Apostolic Letter of Pope Paul VI, 1971.

8. *Justice in the World*. Statement of the Synod of Bishops, 1971.

9. *Evangelization in the Modern World (Evangelli Nuntiandi)*. Apostolic Exhortation of Pope Paul VI, 1975.

10. *On Human Work (Laborem Exercens)*. Encyclical Letter of Pope John Paul II, 1981.

11. *The Social Concerns of the Church (Sollicitudo Rei Socialis)*. Encyclical Letter of Pope John Paul II, 1988.

12. *The Challenge of Peace: God's Promise and Our Response*. Pastoral Letter of the National Conference of Catholic Bishops, United States, 1983.

13. *Economic Justice for All: Catholic Social Teaching and the U.S. Economy*. Pastoral Letter of the National Conference of Catholic Bishops, United States, 1986.

14. *To the Ends of the Earth*. Pastoral Statement of the National Conference of Catholic Bishops, United States, 1986.

15. *The Medellín Conference Documents*. Second meeting of the Latin American Episcopal Conference, 1968.

16. *The Puebla Conference Document*. Third meeting of the Latin American Episcopal Conference, 1979.

17. *Justice and Evangelization in Africa*. Statement of the Symposium of Episcopal Conferences of Africa, Madagascar, 1981.

18. *Evangelization in Modern Day Asia*. First Plenary Assembly of the Federation of Asian Bishops' Conferences, Taiwan, 1974.

These documents, obviously, are not the only examples of the Church's social teaching. They were chosen because they are outstanding examples of the development of the themes of peace and justice.

The first eleven documents are generally considered to be the primary documents among the social teaching from recent Popes, Vatican II, and the Synods of Bishops. A further listing of important Roman documents of the past two decades would also include Vatican II's *On Religious Freedom* (1965); Pope John Paul II's *Redeemer of Humankind* (*Redemptor Hominis*, 1979) and *Rich in Mercy* (*Dives Misericordiae*, 1980); the Congregation for the Defense of Faith's two instructions (1984 and 1986) on the theology of liberation; and the Pontifical Justice and Peace Commission's *An Ethical Approach to the International Debt Question* (1987).

The remaining six documents are examples of significant statements of regional and national conferences of Bishops around the world. As the Church's social teaching continues to develop, local statements such as these will assume ever greater importance in the articulation of authentic teaching related to concrete situations.

The numbers in parentheses at the end of the sentences in the outlines which follow refer to the paragraph numbers of the text of the original documents. These may be used to locate the full development of the points which are made in the outline.

1

THE CONDITION OF LABOR

Rerum Novarum, Encyclical Letter of Pope Leo XIII, 1891

> **Major Areas of Concern**
> —Care for the Poor
> —Rights of Workers
> —Role of Private Property
> —Duties of Workers and Employers
> —Return to Christian Morals
> —Role of Public Authority

In this encyclical Pope Leo XIII examines the situation of the poor people and workers in industrialized countries. He states several important principles that should guide the response to these people. He then articulates the role of the Church, workers and employers, and the law and public authorities in working together to build a just society. Employers are given the major role as agents for change.

HISTORICAL NOTE

The terrible exploitation and poverty of European and North American workers at the end of the nineteenth century prompted the writing of *The Condition of Labor*. The document was inspired by the work of the Fribourg Union, a Catholic Social Action movement in Germany, and by request from the hierarchy in England, Ireland, and the United States.

A. The Situation of the Poor and Workers
1. Destitution of the masses and the wealth of a few (#1).
2. Decline of public morality (#2).
3. Workers exploited by greedy employers (#6).
4. Public authorities *not* protecting the rights of the poor (#6).

B. Guiding Principles
1. All have been created by, strive toward, and have been redeemed by God; divine grace and the goods of nature belong equally to all (#'s 11, 12, 38).
2. Natural inequalities in talents exist among people, but God has gifted all with equal dignity (#26).
3. Ability to reason is part of human nature; humans rule themselves by reason (#'s 11–12).
4. Common good is the end of civil society; all have the right to participate in society (#71).
5. True dignity resides in moral living; people of virtue will have eternal happiness (#'s 37, 42).
6. "Laws are to be obeyed only insofar as they conform with right reason and the eternal law of God" (#72).
7. National wealth originates from the labor of workers (#51).
8. All have the right to own private property (Leo criticized socialism as inherently unjust for violating this right); private property must serve the common good (#'s 2, 9, 10, 15, 23, 36, 55).
9. People have the right to the fruits of their labor but should use them to benefit all (#14).
10. Labor is necessary and there will be hardships in life (#62).
11. Wealth is a hindrance to eternal life (#34).
12. Just ownership is distinct from just use of property (#35).

C. Role of the Church
1. The Church has the right to speak out; social matters affect religion and morality (#24).

2. Through use of Gospel principles the Church can help reconcile and unify classes (#'s 25, 33, 41).
3. The Church can educate people to act justly (#'s 40, 42).

D. Rights and Duties of Workers/Poor and Employers/Wealthy of Society (#'s 30–32)

1. Workers/Poor

    a. Rights: private property, poor must be cared for, possess fruits of their labor, rights of families, freedom of action, right to work, just wage (enough to support a family), join workers associations (which uphold religious values) (#'s 5, 9, 48, 55, 62, 63, 69).

    b. Duties: to work well, not to harm property of employer, to refrain from violence and rioting, to be thrifty (#30).

2. Employers/Wealthy

    a. Rights: private property, no crushing taxes, private societies (#'s 8, 9, 36, 72).

    b. Duties: not to treat workers as slaves, uphold dignity of workers, let workers attend to their religious and family obligations, not to impose more work than a person's strength can endure, pay a just wage, not to tamper with worker's savings, to give to the poor after needs have been met (#'s 31–32).

E. Role of Public Authority and Law in Society

1. Defend and foster the rights of families (#21).
2. Support the common good (#4).
3. Safeguard well-being and rights of non-owning workers (#49).
4. Intervene when necessary to prevent harm to individuals or the common good (#52).
5. Give special consideration to the rights of the poor (#'s 51, 54).
6. Uphold rights of private property and enable all to possess private property (#'s 55, 65).
7. Uphold the rights of associations and the religious rights of people (#69).

2

THE RECONSTRUCTION
OF THE SOCIAL ORDER

*Quadragesimo Anno, Encyclical
Letter of Pope Pius XI, 1931*

Major Areas of Concern
—Role of the Church
—Responsible Ownership
—Labor and Capital
—Public Authority
—Just Social Order
—Capitalism and Socialism

Pope Pius XI covers three major areas in his encyclical. First, he describes the impact of Leo XIII's *The Condition of Labor* on the Church, civil authorities, and other concerned parties. Secondly, Pius clarifies and develops the social and economic doctrine contained in *The Condition of Labor*. He articulates a positive role for the Church in economic and social affairs and affirms the social responsibility of ownership. He advocates a unity between capital and labor and urges the uplifting of the poor and a reform of the social order based on a reestablishment of vocational groups. Finally, Pius treats the abuses of capitalism and socialism and calls for the moral renovation of society coupled with action for justice based on love.

HISTORICAL NOTE

The Reconstruction of the Social Order commemorates the fortieth anniversary of *The Condition of Labor*. Pius wrote and issued this encyclical during a time when major depression was shaking the economic and social foundations in society worldwide. He strongly criticized the abuses of both capitalism and communism and attempted to update Catholic social teaching to reflect changed conditions. He broadened the Church's concern for poor workers to encompass the structures which oppress them.

Part One: Impact of *The Condition of Labor*

I. On the Church
A. Doctrine
1. Encouraged adaptability to changing conditions (#18).
2. Committed many priests and lay people to the Church's social teaching (#19).
3. Inspired a truly Christian social science (#20).
4. Taught in seminars and universities (#20).
5. Has influence outside the Church (#21).

B. Practical Application
1. Effort to help lower classes (#23).
2. Influenced education and culture (#23).
3. Works of charity multiplied (#24).
4. Inspired institutions for mutual support (#24).

II. On Civil Authority
1. Defined positive role: to protect law and order and to promote public well-being (#25).
2. Government must have a special regard for the infirm and needy (#25).
3. Leaders became more conscious of their obligations to promote social policy (#26).
4. Laws and programs for the poor were begun (#28).

III. On Other Concerned Parties
  #### A. Unions
  1. Confirmed their mission (#31).
  2. Clergy and laity helped create them (#33).
  3. Unions have flourished (#33).
  4. Leo XIII's counsels should be adapted to different situations (#34).
  #### B. Other
  1. Associations of employers did not meet with much success (#38).
  2. Leo drew his inspiration from the Gospel (#39).

Part Two: Social and Economic Doctrine

  #### A. Role of the Church (#41)
  1. Church has a right and duty to deal with these issues.
  2. It is a "God given task".
  3. Church must pass judgment on social and economic questions as they affect moral issues.
  #### B. Property Rights
  1. Two-fold aspect of ownership: individual and social (concerns for the common good) (#45).
  2. Double danger: individualism and collectivism (#46).
  3. Right of property must be distinguished from its use (#47).
  4. To destroy the individual character of ownership is a grievous error (#48).
  5. Right of ownership is not absolute (#49).
  6. Function of government: to define in detail the duties of ownership (#49).
  7. Two uses of superfluous income:
     a. charity (#50);
     b. to create employment (#51).
  #### C. Capital and Labor
  1. Only by the labor of working people does the state grow rich (#53).
  2. Labor and capital need each other (#53).
  3. In history, capital claimed all the products and profits and left the barest minimum to labor (#54).

    4. Unjust claim of labor: all products and profit belong to working people (#55).

    5. Advocates a just distribution of wealth to serve the common good (#56).

D. Uplifting the Proletariat

    1. Uplifting the proletariat is the main objective (#59).

    2. The situation of workers has improved in Western nations (#59).

    3. But the situation has deteriorated in other parts of the world (#60).

    4. Condition of rural laborers is extremely depressed (#60).

    5. Working people should be sufficiently supplied with fruits of productions (#61).

    6. A just wage should be paid so people can acquire moderate ownership (#63).

    7. The idea of a wage contract is not necessarily unjust (#64).

    8. Wage contract should be modified by a contract of partnerships (#65).

    9. Demand of social justice: wages should support families (#71).

    10. Women and children should not be abused in the work world (#71).

    11. Public authorities can help businesses pay a just wage (#73).

    12. Opportunities must be provided to those willing to work (#74).

E. Reform of Social Order

    1. This is primarily the State's responsibility (#78).

    2. Principles of subsidiarity: activity that can be performed by a more decentralized entity should be (#'s 79–80).

    3. Primary duty of the State: to abolish conflict and promote harmony between classes (#81).

    4. Importance of vocational groups: common effort for the common good (#84).

    5. Proper ordering of economic affairs cannot be left to free enterprise alone (#88).

6. Economic supremacy has replaced free competition (#88).
7. Economic institutions must be imbued with a spirit of justice (#89).
8. Calls for international economic cooperation (#89).
9. Supports public intervention in labor-management disputes (#93).

Part Three: Socialism

A. Changes in Capitalism
1. Economic concentration has led to a struggle for domination (#105).
2. Free competition has ended (#109).
3. State has become a "slave" serving greed (#109).
4. Economic imperialism thrives (#109).

B. Changes in Socialism
1. Divided into two camps (#111).
2. Communism supports violence and the abolition of private ownership (#112).
3. Socialism condemns the resort to physical force and moderates the prohibition on private property (#113).

C. Remedies
1. No possibility of a compromise between Christianity and Socialism (#116).
2. Socialism perceives humans in a way alien to Christian truth (#118).
3. Social reconstruction needs a return to Christian spirit and Gospel principles (#136).
4. Love and charity must reinforce justice (#137).

3

CHRISTIANITY AND SOCIAL PROGRESS

Mater et Magistra, Encyclical Letter of Pope John XXIII, 1961

> **Major Areas of Concern**
> —Just Remuneration
> —Subsidiarity
> —Agriculture
> —Economic Development
> —Role of the Church
> —International Cooperation
> —Socialization

Pope John XXIII begins this encyclical by reviewing the major points of *The Condition of Labor* and *The Reconstruction of the Social Order*. He notes that new political, social, and economic developments have necessitated *Christianity and Social Progress*. He confirms previous papal teaching on the value of private initiative, just remuneration for work, and the social function of private property. John XXIII then treats the questions of agriculture and aid to developing countries. He urges a reconstruction of social relationships according to the principles of Catholic social teaching and states the responsibility of individual Christians to work for a more just world.

HISTORICAL NOTE

Pope John XXIII issued *Christianity and Social Progress* in response to the severe imbalances between the rich and the poor which exist in the world. The encyclical commemorates the seventieth anniversary of Leo XIII's *The Condition of Labor*. John XXIII "internationalizes" the Catholic social teaching by treating, for the first time, the situation of countries which are not fully industrialized. He articulates an important role for the laity in applying the Church's social teachings in the world.

I. New Developments

A. Economic and Scientific (#47)
1. Discovery of atomic energy.
2. Synthetic products and automation.
3. Conquest of outer space.
4. New speed of transportation.
5. Improvements in communications.

B. Social (#48)
1. Insurance and social security.
2. Improvements in education.
3. Increased social mobility.
4. Pronounced imbalances between more developed and less developed areas.

C. Political (#49)
1. Increased participation.
2. Less colonization.
3. More public intervention.

II. Development of Social Teaching

A. Private Initiative
1. First priority to private initiative (#51).
2. Supports principle of "subsidiarity" (#53).

3. Public authorities can intervene to reduce economic imbalances (#54).
4. Balance between public and private initiative (#55).
5. "Socialization": interdependent social relationships with positive and negative consequences created by new developments (#'s 59–67).

B. Just Remuneration for Work
1. Families need appropriate wage to live in dignity (#68).
2. World imbalance: too much money spent on national prestige and armaments (#69).
3. Economic development must correspond to social development (#73).
4. Economic prosperity: the just and proper distribution of goods (#74).
5. Workers should share in running of companies (management, profits, ownership) (#75).
6. Requirements for common good for nations (#79):
   a. create employment;
   b. care for less privileged;
   c. provide for the future.

C. Justice and Productive Institutions
1. Foster small and intermediary holdings (#84).
2. Encourage family-type ownership (#85).
3. Alleviate imbalances (#84).
4. All should work for the common good (#96).

D. Private Property
1. Confirms rights to private property (#109).
2. Encourages widespread ownership (#115).
3. State can own means of production (but affirms subsidiarity) (#117).
4. Social responsibility: a function of private property (#119).

III. New Aspects of the Social Question

A. Agriculture
1. Agriculture is a depressed sector; imbalances between it and industry exist (#123).
2. Church calls for services for rural areas and orderly economic development (#127).

3. Appropriate economic policy includes capital at suitable prices, price protection, social security, and strengthening farm income (#'s 131–143).
4. Principal agent for improvement should be rural workers, who have dignity from God (#144).

B. Aid to Less Developed Areas

1. Need for competent administration and economic policies (#150).
2. Citizens in less developed areas are chiefly responsible for their own development and need to respect dignity and subsidiarity (#151).

C. Justice between Nations Differing in Development

1. Peace is more difficult as imbalances persist (#157).
2. Duty of countries to help the poor and unfortunate (#157).
3. Need to establish an effective program of emergency assistance (#161).
4. Private enterprises and societies need to be more generous in cooperation (#165).
5. Industrial countries need to respect the culture of developing countries; aid should be offered without the intent to dominate (#'s 170, 172).

D. Role of the Church

1. Individual Christians must advance civil institutions and human dignity and foster a unity between peoples (#179).
2. Many Catholics are already involved in these efforts (#182).

E. Population Increase and Development

1. Humankind has an inexhaustible productive capacity (#189).
2. Humans should not resort to means of population control beneath human dignity (#199).

F. International Cooperation

1. Relationships are interdependent; cooperation and mutual assistance are needed (#200).
2. Cause of distrust is failure to agree on laws of justice; armaments are a symptom of this distrust (#203).

IV. Reconstruction of Social Relationships

A. Incomplete Philosophies of Life
1. Many philosophies do not encompass the entire human person or respect human dignity (#'s 213–214).
2. It is folly to establish a temporal order without God as a foundation (#217).

B. Catholic Social Teaching (CST)
1. Individuals are the foundation, cause, and end of all social institutions (#219).
2. CST cannot be separated from Church teachings on life and should be taught at all levels and in the media (#'s 222–223).
3. Catholics should be reared on CST and conform their social and economic behavior to CST principles (#228).
4. Applying CST in the world is difficult (#229).
5. How to apply CST (task for laity) (#'s 236–241):
   a. examine situation (observe);
   b. evaluate it with respect to CST (judge);
   c. decide how to act (act).

C. Conclusion
1. Industrial life can deform values and depart from human dignity (#242).
2. Church needs to renew its dedication in seeking to establish the Kingdom in temporal affairs (#254).

4

PEACE ON EARTH

Pacem in Terris, Encyclical Letter of Pope John XXIII, 1963

Major Areas of Concern
—Rights and Duties
—Role of Public Authorities
—Common Good
—Christian World Order
—International Relations
—Disarmament

In *Peace on Earth*, Pope John XXIII contends that peace can be established only if the social order set down by God is fully observed. Relying extensively on reason and the natural law tradition, John XXIII sketches a list of rights and duties to be followed by individuals, public authorities, national governments, and the world community. Peace needs to be based on an order "founded on truth, built according to justice, vivified and integrated by charity, and put into practice in freedom."

HISTORICAL NOTE

Written during the first year of Vatican II, *Peace on Earth* was the first encyclical addressed to "all people of good will." Issued shortly after the Cuban Missile Crisis in 1962 and the erection of the Berlin Wall, this document spoke to a world aware of the dangers of nuclear war. Its optimistic tone and development of a philosophy of rights made a significant impression on Catholics and non-Catholics alike.

I. Order between People
Every human is a person, endowed with intelligence and free will, who has universal and inviolable rights and duties (#9).

A. Rights
1. Rights to life and worthy standard of living, including rights to proper development of life and to basic security (#11).
2. Rights of cultural and moral values, including freedom to search for and express opinions, freedom of information, and right to education (#'s 12–13).
3. Rights to religion and conscience (#14).
4. Rights to choose one's state in life, including rights to establish a family and pursue a religious vocation (#'s 15–16).
5. Economic rights, including right to work, to a just and sufficient wage, and to hold private property (#'s 18–22).
6. Rights of meeting and association (#23).
7. Right to emigrate and immigrate (#25).
8. Political rights, including right to participate in public affairs and juridical protection of rights (#'s 26–27).

B. Duties
1. To acknowledge and respect rights of others (#30).
2. To collaborate mutually (#31).
3. To act for others responsibly (#39).
4. To preserve life and live it becomingly (#42).

C. Signs of the Times

1. Working classes have gradually gained ground in economic and social affairs (#40).
2. Women are participating in public life (#41).
3. All nations are becoming independent (#42).

II. Relations between Individuals and Public Authorities in a Single State

A. Nature of Authority

1. Authority is necessary for the proper functioning of society (#46).
2. It derives its force from the moral order which has God for its end (#47).
3. A state which uses, as its chief means, punishments and rewards cannot effectively promote the common good (#48).
4. A state cannot oblige in matters of conscience (#49).
5. A command contrary to God's will is not binding (#51).

B. Characteristics of Common Good

1. Human person must be considered (#55).
2. All members of the state share in common good (#56).
3. More attention must be given to the less fortunate members of society (#56).
4. State must promote material and spiritual welfare of citizens (#57).

C. Civil Authority

1. Chief concern should be to ensure the common good (#59).
2. Coordinates social relations in a way that allows people to exercise their rights and duties peacefully (#60).
3. A three-fold division of powers—legislative, executive, and judicial—is recommended for public authorities (#68).
4. Often a prudent and thoughtful juridical system seems inadequate for society's needs (#71).
5. Three requisites for good government:
   a. charter of human rights (#75);
   b. written constitution (#76);

c. relations between governed and government in terms of rights and duties (#77).

III. Relations between States

A. In Truth
1. Elimination of racism (#86).
2. Right to self-development (#86).
3. Obligation of mutual assistance (#87).
4. Objective use of media (#90).

B. In Justice
1. Recognition of mutual rights and duties (#91).
2. Improvement of the situation of ethnic minorities (#96).

C. Active Solidarity
1. Promote by civil authority the common good of the entire human family (#98).
2. Fostering of friendly relations in all fields (#100).
3. Reduction in imbalances of goods and capital in the world (#101).
4. Right of political refugees to migrate (#106).
5. Arms race:
   a. deprives less developed countries of social and economic progress (#109);
   b. creates a climate of fear (#111);
   c. "Justice, then, right reason, and consideration for human dignity and life demand that the arms race cease" (#112);
   d. peace consists in mutual trust (#114).

D. In Liberty
1. Relations based on freedom; responsibility and enterprise encouraged (#120).
2. Respect by the wealthy nations of the value in giving aid without seeking dominance (#125).

IV. Relations of People and of Political Communities with the World Community

1. Individual countries cannot seek their own interests and develop in isolation given modern conditions of interdependence (#131).

2. Under present circumstances, the structures and forms of national governments are inadequate to promote the universal common good (#135).
3. Public authority must have the means to promote the common good (#136).
4. Need public authority to operate in an effective matter on a world-wide matter (#137).
5. The United Nations should be fostered (#145).

V. Pastoral Exhortations

1. People should take an active role in public life and organizations and influence them from within (#147).
2. Humans should carry on temporal activities "as acts within the moral order" (#150).
3. A unity between faith and action is needed; solid Christian education will help achieve this unity (#'s 152–153).
4. Distinguish between false philosophical ideas and movements deriving from them (#159).
5. Christians need prudence in determining when to collaborate with non-Christians in social and economic affairs (#160).
6. "Peace will be but an empty sounding word unless it is founded on the order which the present document has outlined in confident hope: an order founded on truth, built according to justice, vivified and integrated by charity, and put into practice in freedom" (#167).

5

THE CHURCH IN THE MODERN WORLD

Gaudium et Spes, Second Vatican Council, 1965

Major Areas of Concern
—Human Dignity
—Common Good
—"Signs of the Times"
—Public Responsibility
—Respect for Families
—Right of Culture
—Justice and Development
—Peace

Vatican II's *The Church in the Modern World* is seen by many to be the most important document in the Church's social tradition. It announces the duty of the People of God to scrutinize the "signs of the times" in light of the Gospel. In doing so, it finds that change characterizes the world. These technological and social changes provide both wonderful opportunities and worrisome difficulties for the spread of the Gospel. The Church's duty in the world is to work for the enhancement of human dignity and the common good.

HISTORICAL NOTE

This document represents the opinion of the overwhelming majority of the world's Bishops. Originally, the material contained here was not scheduled to be considered separately by the Council. Cardinal Joseph Suenens of Belgium, however, intervened at the end of the first session to urge consideration of issues more "external" to the Church than the role of Bishops or the use of vernacular in the liturgy. The document is the product of a commission and was altered by a 2,300 member deliberative assembly. In final form, it represents a significant break from the rigid traditionalism of the Council's preparatory commission.

Introduction
    A. The "joys and hopes, sorrows and anxieties" of the people of the world are the concerns of the People of God (#1).

    B. Church's duty: to scrutinize the "signs of the times" (#4).
        1. Technological changes have caused social changes (#5).
        2. These changes have affected everybody—individuals, families, communities, and nations—with both good and bad results (#'s 6–7).
        3. Conflicting forces have ensued: tremendous wealth and abject poverty, great freedom and psychological slavery (#9).
        4. Conviction has grown that humanity can establish a political order that will serve human dignity (#9).

Part One: The Church and Humanity's Calling

I. Human Dignity
    A. Nature of Human
        1. Created in God's image (free and intelligent), and as a social being (#12).

2. Split within self: inclination toward good and evil (#13).
3. Dignity depends on freedom to obey one's conscience (#16).

B. Christianity and Atheism

1. Atheism: a serious concern, impeding the liberation of the complete person and antagonistic toward religion (#19).
2. But recognition of God is in no way hostile to human dignity (#21).
3. A living faith, activating people to justice and love, is needed to overcome suspicion of religion (#21).
4. Church calls for all to work to better the world; this work corresponds to the work of the human heart (#21).

C. Human Community

1. Technological changes have created interdependence without fostering interpersonal relationships (#23).
2. Advancement of individuals and society depends on everyone (#25).
3. All must work for the common good (#26).
4. Everything necessary for a truly human life must be made available for us (#26).
5. Scripture mandates love of neighbor; every person is our neighbor; active love is necessary (#28).
6. Jesus calls us God's children so we should treat each other as sisters and brothers (#32).

D. The Church in the Modern World

1. The Church and humanity experience the same earthly situation (#40).
2. History, science, and culture reveal the true nature of the human person (#41).
3. The Church is not bound to any particular political, economic, or social system (#42).
4. The Church needs to purify itself continually (#43).
5. Individual Christians need to penetrate the world with a Christian spirit and witness to Jesus in the midst of human society (#43).
6. The Church can be helped by the world in preparing the ground for the Gospel (#44).

7. The Church's mission, part saving and eschatological, begins in this world; Jesus is Lord of history (#45).

Part Two: Special Areas of Concern

I. Marriage and the Family
1. Families are the foundation of society (#47).
2. Destructive to marriage are: divorce, free love, excessive self-love, polygamy, worship of pleasure, certain modern economic-social-political conditions, overpopulation (#47).
3. Marriage is intended for the procreation and education of children and a whole manner and communion of life (#50).
4. Responsible parenthood is advocated (#50).
5. From the moment of conception, life must be regarded with sacred care (#51).
6. The healthy condition of individuals and society depends on stable families (#52).

II. The Development of Culture
A. Circumstances of Culture
1. Changes in technology have created fresh avenues for the diffusion of culture (#54).
2. A new humanism has dawned and an individual is defined by his/her responsibilities to the world (#55).
3. Culture must evolve so as to foster the development of the whole person (#56).

B. Principles of Cultural Development
1. The quest for heaven should inspire Christians to build a more human world on earth (#57).
2. Danger exists that humans may rely on modern discoveries and stop searching for higher realities (#57).
3. God speaks to the various cultures (#58).
4. Church, in ways that respect its own tradition, should use modes of culture to spread the Gospel (#58).
5. The Good News renews and advances culture (#58).
6. Culture needs freedom in which to develop (#59).

C. Cultural Duties of Christians

1. Strenuous work is needed in economic and political fields to liberate people from ignorance (#60).
2. Everyone has a right to culture, thought, and expression (#60).
3. Women should participate in cultural life (#60).
4. Development of the whole person should be fostered (#61).
5. Christian thinking should be expressed in ways consistent with culture (#62).

III. Socio-Economic Life

A. Basic Principles

1. Human beings are "the source, the center, and the purpose of all socio-economic life" (#63).
2. Fundamental imbalances between wealth and poverty exist in today's world (#63).

B. Economic Development

1. Technological progress which serves the whole person must be fostered (#64).
2. Progress must be controlled by humanity (#65).
3. Justice necessitates a quick removal of economic inequities (#66).

C. Economic Life

1. Human labor is superior to other elements of economic life; economic activity detrimental to the worker is wrong and inhuman (#67).
2. Workers should participate in running an enterprise (#67).
3. God intended the earth for everyone; private property should benefit all (#67).
4. All have a right to goods sufficient for themselves and their families (#69).
5. Distribution of goods should be directed toward employment (#70).
6. Public authorities can guard against those misuses of private property which hurt the common good (#71).
7. Genuine sharing of goods is called for (#71).

IV. Political Community

1. Modern changes have increased the awareness of human dignity and the desire to establish a just political-juridical order (#73).
2. Public authorities (and individual citizens) should work for the common good (#74).
3. Church and political community (#76):
   a. both serve the vocation of humans;
   b. Church has the right to pass moral judgments when human rights are at stake;
   c. Church should use the means of the Gospel to fulfill its mission.

V. Peace

A. Basic Principles

1. With modern weapons, humanity is in a crisis situation (#77).
2. Most noble meaning of "peace"—based on love, harmony, trust, and justice—should be fostered (#78).

B. Avoidance of War

1. Non-violence and conscientious objection are legitimate (#79).
2. Just defense is permissible, but not wars of subjugation (#79).
3. Participation in armed services is allowed but not blind obedience to orders (#79).
4. With new weapons, a new evaluation of war is needed (#80).
5. Arms race is not the way to build peace; it can actually foster wars and it injures the poor (#81).
6. No act of war at population centers is permissible (#81).
7. Deterrence "is not a safe way to preserve steady peace" (#81).
8. Everyone has responsibility to work for disarmament (#82).

C. Building Up the International Community

1. Causes of dissension, especially injustices, need to be eliminated (#83).

2. Greater international cooperation demands the establishment of an international organization corresponding to modern obligations (#'s 84–85).
3. Development of whole person is to be fostered (#86).
4. Ecumenical cooperation is needed to achieve justice (#88).
5. Church must be present to injustice (#89).

6

THE DEVELOPMENT OF
PEOPLES

*Populorum Progressio, Encyclical
Letter of Pope Paul VI, 1967*

Major Areas of Concern
—Human Aspirations
—Structural Injustice
—Church and Development
—New Humanism
—Common Good
—Economic Planning
—International Trade
—Peace

In *The Development of Peoples*, Pope Paul VI speaks to the challenge of development. He explores the nature of poverty and the conflicts it produces. He articulates the role of the Church in the process of development and sketches a Christian vision of development. The Pope calls for urgent action which respects the universal purpose of created things. He advocates economic planning and aid to promote development. Paul VI urges equity in trade relations as well as universal charity. He concludes by terming "development" the new name for peace and exhorts all Christians to strive for justice.

HISTORICAL NOTE

In this encyclical, Paul VI enlarges the scope of Leo XIII's treatment of the struggle between the rich and poor classes to encompass the conflict between rich and poor nations. *The Development of Peoples* is the first encyclical devoted entirely to the international development issue. The Pope stresses the economic sources of war and highlights economic justice as the basis of peace. More so than any of his predecessors, Paul VI explicitly criticizes basic tenets of capitalism, including the profit motive and the unrestricted right of private property.

I. Humanity's Complete Development

A. The Data of the Problem
 1. Human aspirations include (#6):
    a. freedom from misery;
    b. assurance of finding subsistence;
    c. responsibility without oppression;
    d. better education.
 2. The means inherited from the past are not lacking but are insufficient for the present situation (#7).
 3. Social conflicts now have a worldwide dimension (#9).
 4. Structures have not adapted themselves to the new conditions (#10).

B. The Church and Development
 1. Responding to the teaching of Jesus, the Church must foster human progress (#12).
 2. World demands action based on a vision of the economic, social, cultural, and spiritual aspects of the situation (#13).
 3. The Church was "founded to establish on earth the Kingdom of Heaven" (#13).

4. Development cannot be limited to economic growth but looks to total human potential (#14).

5. People have a right and a duty to develop themselves; as beings with a spiritual dimension, people should orient their lives to God, creating a transcendent humanism (#15–16).

6. Each person is a member of society (#17).

7. Work is a necessity but greed must be avoided (#18).

8. Avarice is the most blatant form of moral underdevelopment (#19).

9. A new humanism which embraces higher values of love, friendship, prayer, and contemplation is needed for a full and authentic development (#20).

C. Action to be undertaken

1. Universal purpose of created things:
   a. God intends the earth and its goods for use by everyone; all other rights must be subordinated to this (#22).
   b. Private property is not an absolute and unconditional right, but must be exercised for the common good; public authority must ensure this and the common good sometimes requires expropriation (#'s 23–24).

2. Industrialization.
   a. Industry is necessary for economic growth and progress (#25).
   b. Structures of capitalism—profit, competition, and absolute private ownership—are "unfortunate" (#26).
   c. Industrialization can be separated from the capitalistic system (#26).

3. Urgency to the task.
   a. Too many people are suffering; disparity between the rich and poor grows (#29).
   b. With situations of injustice, recourse to violence is a grave temptation(#30).
   c. Cautions against revolutions; greater misery may result (#31).
   d. Present situation must be fought against and overcome (#32).

4. Programs and Planning.
   a. Individual initiative and free competition are not enough; public programs are necessary (#33).
   b. Public authorities must choose objectives and stimulate activity (#33).
   c. Service of humanity is the aim of development (#34).
   d. Economic growth depends on social progress; better education is needed (#35).
   e. Christians should not subscribe to doctrines based on materialistic and atheistic philosophies (#39).
   f. Developing nations should honor their own cultures (#40).
   g. Complete humanism is the aim of development(#42).

II. Development in Solidarity
A. Aid for the Poor
   1. The problem: hunger, malnutrition, stunted physical and mental growth (#45).
   2. Response demands generosity, sacrifice, and efforts by the rich: a solidarity that costs (#46).
   3. Advanced countries should offer financial and educational assistance (#47).
   4. "The superfluous wealth of rich countries should be placed at the service of poor nations" (#49).
   5. Recommendations: support Food and Agriculture Organization; establish a World Fund (money from arms race to aid destitute); worldwide collaboration and dialogue (#52-54).
   6. Public and private squandering of wealth is an intolerable scandal (#53).
B. Equity in Trade Relations
   1. The problem: industrialized nations export primarily manufactured goods; developing nations raw goods; price of manufactured goods is increasing; raw materials are subject to wide price fluctuation; developing nations have great difficulty in balancing their economies (#57).
   2. Free trade is no longer capable of governing international relations (#58).

3. The fundamental principles of liberalism are in question (#58).
4. *The Condition of Labor* held that if the positions of the contracting parties are unequal, the contract is void (#59).
5. Freedom of trade is fair only if it is subject to the demands of social justice (#59).
6. Discussion and negotiation are necessary to reach equality of opportunity (#61).
7. Nationalism and racism are major obstacles of justice (#62).

C. Universal Charity

1. "The world is sick": lack of concern for others (#66).
2. It is the duty of people to welcome others, especially youth and migrant workers (#67).
3. Business people in developing nations should be initiators of social progress and human advancement (#70).
4. Sincere dialogue and affection are needed (#73).

D. Development Is the New Name for Peace

1. Peace is built daily in pursuit of God's order (#76).
2. People themselves have a prime responsibility for their own development.
3. International collaboration on a worldwide scale for justice is needed (#78).
4. The hour for action is now (#80).
5. Role of lay persons: "to infuse a Christian spirit into the mentality, customs, laws and structures" of their communities and nations (#81).
6. Catholics should support development efforts generously (#81).
7. To struggle against injustice is to promote the common good (#82).
8. Peace is not the mere absence of war (#83).

7

A CALL TO ACTION

Octogesima Adveniens, Apostolic Letter of Pope Paul VI, 1971

Major Areas of Concern
—Urbanization
—Role of Local Churches
—Duties of Individual Christians
—Political Activity
—Worldwide Dimensions of Justice

Pope Paul VI begins this letter by urging greater efforts for justice and noting the duties of local churches to respond to specific situations. The Pope then discusses a wide variety of new social problems which stem from urbanization. These issues include women, youth, and the "new poor." Paul VI next treats modern aspirations and ideas, especially liberalism and Marxism. He stresses the need to ensure equality and the right of all to participate in society. He concludes this letter by encouraging all Christians to reflect on their contemporary situations, apply Gospel principles, and take political action when appropriate.

HISTORICAL NOTE

A Call to Action is an open, apostolic letter from Pope Paul VI to Cardinal Maurice Roy, president of the Pontifical Commission on Justice and Peace, to commemorate the eightieth anniversary of the publication of Pope Leo XIII's *The Condition of Labor*. It breaks new ground by developing a theory of the role of individual Christians and local churches in responding to situations of injustices.

A. Introduction
1. Greater efforts for justice are needed (#2).
2. Given the wide diversity of situations in the world, each local church has responsibility to discern and act (#4).
3. A great variety of changes are taking place in the world (#7).

B. New Social Problems
1. Urbanization creates a new loneliness and the possibility that humans may become slaves to their own creation (#10).
2. Youth find dialogue increasingly difficult (#13).
3. Women possess an equal right to participate in social, cultural, economic, and political life (#13).
4. Workers have the right to form unions (#14).
5. The "New Poor," created by urbanization, include the handicapped, elderly, and the marginalized (#15).
6. Discrimination along lines of race, origin, color, culture, sex, and religion still exists (#17).
7. Emigration is a right (#17).
8. There is great need to create employment through effective policies of investment, education, and organization of means of production (#18).
9. The media have both positive and negative potential (#20).

10. People have a responsibility to protect the environment (#21).

C. Fundamental Aspirations and Ideas

1. Equality and participation need to be ensured (#22).
2. Legislation for justice is necessary but not enough; love sparking action for the poor is needed (#23).
3. Preferential respect for the poor is important (#23).
4. Political activity for a democratic society is consistent with the total vocation of humankind; humans can no longer rely only on economic activity (#25).
5. Both Marxist and liberal ideologies alienate human beings (#26).
6. Historical movements contain positive elements which must be discerned (#30).
7. Certain features of socialism are attractive but Christians must critique its appeal (#31).
8. A variety of interpretations of Marxism exist but historically it has led to totalitarianism and violence (#'s 32–34).
9. Liberalism promotes economic efficiency but distorts human nature (#35).
10. Christians need to discern carefully the options between different ideologies (#36).
11. Utopias are generally ineffective but they provoke the imagination and activity for a better world (#37).
12. Humans have become the object of science; science lacks a total picture of humanity (#39).
13. Nature of progress is ambiguous; quality of human relations and degree of participation and responsibility are just as important as amount of goods produced (#41).

D. Christians Face New Problems

1. Catholic social teaching states the importance of reflecting on the changing situation of the world and applying Gospel principles to it (#42).

2. Nations need to revise their relationships to work for greater justice (#43).
3. Liberation requires changed attitudes and structures (#45).
4. The task of Christians is to create conditions for the complete good of humanity (#46).
5. Christians need to concentrate more on political rather than economic activity as a solution for contemporary problems (#46).
6. Involvement in building human solidarity is an end of freedom (#47).

E. Call to Action

1. Each Christian has a personal responsibility for building up the temporal order (#48).
2. The Lord working with us is a great reason for Christian hope (#48).
3. A plurality of options for action exists (#49).
4. Christians have the task of inspiring and innovating in working for justice (#50).

8

JUSTICE IN THE WORLD

Statement of the Synod of Bishops, 1971

Major Areas of Concern
—Gospel Mandate for Justice
—Right to Development
—Justice as Christian Love
—Education for Justice
—International Action

The 1971 Synod of Bishops, in their reflection on "the mission of the People of God to further justice in the world," affirms the right to a culturally-sensitive, personalized development. The Bishops teach that Gospel principles mandate justice for the liberation of all humanity as an essential expression of Christian love. The Church must witness for justice through its own lifestyle, educational activities, and international action. Structural sin is discussed.

HISTORICAL NOTE

This document illustrates the powerful influence of native leadership of the Churches of Africa, Asia, and Latin America. It is the first major example of post-Vatican II episcopal collegiality and reflects a forceful, concrete, and realistic refinement of previous papal pronouncements.

Introduction

1. Structural injustices oppress humanity and stifle freedom to operate in the world (#3).
2. The dynamism of the Gospel and the hopes of the people of today are together (#5).
3. "Action on behalf of justice and participation in the transformation of the world fully appear to us as a constitutive dimension of the preaching of the Gospel, or in other words, of the Church's mission for the redemption of the human race and its liberation from every oppressive situation" (#6).

I. Justice and World Society

1. A modern paradox:
   a. forces for achieving human dignity seem strong (#7);
   b. but so do forces of division (arms race, economic injustices, lack of participation) (#9).
2. Affirms the right to development as a basic human right (#15).
3. Calls for personalization and a culturally-sensitive modernization (#'s 17–19).
4. Many who suffer injustice are voiceless; the Church should speak on their behalf (#20).
5. Injustices listed: those to migrants, refugees; religious persecution; human rights violations; torture; political prisoners; anti-life; war; dishonest media; anti-family activity (#'s 21–26).
6. Dialogue with the participation of all, especially youth, is needed to correct these injustices (#28).

II. Gospel Message and Mission of Christ
A. Scriptural Sources

1. People need to listen to the Word of God to respond effectively to injustices (#29).

2. Old Testament views God as a "liberator of the oppressed and the defender of the poor" (#30).
3. Jesus gave himself for the salvation and liberation of all and associated himself with the "least" (#31).
4. St. Paul: Christian life is the faith which sparks love and service of neighbors (#33).

B. Justice and Love

1. "Christian love of neighbor and justice cannot be separated" (#34).
2. Preaching the Gospel requires a dedication to the liberation of humanity in this world (#35).

C. Role of the Church

1. The Gospel message gives the Church the right and duty to proclaim justice on all levels and to denounce instances of injustice (#36).
2. The role of the hierarchical Church is not to offer concrete solutions to specific problems, but to promote the dignity and rights of each human being (#37).

III. Practice of Justice

A. Witness of the Church

1. Anyone who ventures to preach justice should be perceived as being just (#40).
2. Rights within the Church must be respected for all, especially women and lay people (#43).
3. Rights include: decent wage, security, promotion, freedom of thought and expression, proper judicial procedures, participation in decision-making process (#'s 45–46).
4. The lifestyle of the institutional Church and all its members must allow it to preach the good news to the poor (#48).

B. Education to Justice

1. In developing countries, the aim is to awaken awareness of the concrete situation and strategies and alternatives for change (#51).
2. Family is the principal agent for this education, a continuing one (#54).

  3. Catholic social teaching, the basic principles of the Gospels applied, is the major source for justice education (#56).

  4. Liturgy and the sacraments can serve justice education (#58).

C. Cooperation between Churches in Rich and Poor Nations Is Essential for Economic and Spiritual Progress (#59).

D. Ecumenical Collaboration for Justice Is Strongly Supported (#61).

E. International Action

  1. Call for the UN Declaration of Human Rights to be ratified by all nations (#64).

  2. Support UN efforts to halt arms race, weapons trade, and reach peaceful conflict resolution (#65).

  3. Foster aims of the Second Development Decade, including fair prices for raw materials, opening of markets, taxation on worldwide basis (#66).

  4. Concentration of power should be changed; more participation is needed (#67).

  5. Emphasizes the importance of UN specialized agencies in promoting justice (#68).

  6. Calls for funding for responsible development (#69).

  7. Wealthy nations need to be less materialistic and consume less (#70).

  8. Right to development and respectful cooperation with wealthy nations are urged (#71).

IV. A Word of Hope

  Christians will find the Kingdom as the fruit of their nature and efforts; God is now preparing the Kingdom (#75).

9

EVANGELIZATION IN THE MODERN WORLD

Evangelii Nuntiandi, Apostolic Exhortation of Pope Paul VI, 1975

Major Areas of Concern
—Personal Conversion
—Church and Culture
—Justice and Liberation
—Universal and Individual Churches
—Gospel and Non-Christians

Evangelization in the Modern World represents Pope Paul VI's main teachings on the Church's evangelizing mission. The Pope treats the responsibility of the Church to proclaim the good news in ways that people of the twentieth century can understand. All Christians are urged to spread the Gospel. The Pope declares that combating injustices and preaching liberation constitute essential elements of evangelization.

HISTORICAL NOTE

Commemorating the tenth anniversary of the closing of the Second Vatican Council, *Evangelization in the Modern World* affirms the Council's teachings on the active role that the institutional Church and individual Christians must play in promoting justice in the world. This apostolic exhortation was written at the request of the 1974 Synod of Bishops, which had considered the topic of evangelization but did not produce any major document on it.

Introduction

1. Objective: To make the twentieth-century Church better fitted for proclaiming the Gospel (#2).
2. The Church needs to preserve the heritage of faith and present it in the most persuasive and understandable way possible (#3).

I. Evangelizers: Christ and the Church

1. Mission of Jesus: going from town to town preaching the good news to the poorest (#6).
2. Jesus proclaimed the Kingdom of God and a salvation which is liberation from all oppression (#9).
3. A radical conversion is needed to gain the Kingdom (#10).
4. Jesus proclaimed the Kingdom with signs as well as words (#12).
5. The good news is meant for all people of all times (#13).
6. Evangelizing is "the grace and vocation proper to the Church" (#14).
7. The Church is sent by Jesus and begins by evangelizing itself (#15).

II. Evangelization: The Elements

1. Purpose: To bring the good news "into all strata of humanity," transforming it from within and making it new (#18).

2. Evangelization should affect human judgment, values, interests, thought, and way of life (#19).

3. The Gospel is independent of, but not incompatible with, culture; evangelization of culture is needed (#20).

4. Personal witness and explicit proclamation are needed for evangelization (#21).

5. Evangelization is aided by a community of believers (#23).

III. Evangelization: The Content

1. The primary message: God loves the world and through Jesus salvation is available to all (#'s 26–27).

2. Evangelization has a personal and social dimension involving human rights, peace, justice, development, and liberation (#29).

3. The Church must proclaim liberation (#30).

4. Humans are subject to social and economic questions; the plan of redemption includes combating injustice (#31).

5. Evangelization is a religious as well as a temporal task; Jesus must be proclaimed (#35).

6. The spiritual dimension of liberation is primary; true liberation needs to be motivated by justice and charity (#35).

7. Personal conversion is needed for structural change (#36).

8. The Church cannot accept violence (#37).

9. Religious liberty is an important human right (#39).

IV. Evangelization: The Methods

1. Preaching and the witness of an authentic Christian life are indispensable elements (#'s 41–42).

2. Homilies, catechetical instruction, and mass media also facilitate evangelization (#'s 43–45).

3. Personal contact, the sacraments, and popular piety are also necessary for effective evangelization (#'s 46–48).

V. Evangelization: The Beneficiaries

1. The good news is for everyone (#49).
2. Even today many obstacles (persecution, resistance) impede the spread of the Gospel (#50).
3. "Pre-evangelization" can be an effective aid to the spread of the good news (#51).
4. The Gospel should be proclaimed to non-Christians as well as Christians in our increasingly de-Christianized world (#53).
5. The Church needs to address atheism, humanism, and secularism (#54).
6. Non-practicing Christians should be a special beneficiary of evangelization (#56).
7. There are two kinds of "small communities": one works with the Church, bringing Christians together, and the other bitterly criticizes the Church; the former can be used for evangelization (#58).
8. Small communities need nourishment from the Word and a universal outlook (#58).

VI. Evangelization: The Workers

1. Evangelization is the mission of the Church (#60).
2. Both the universal Church and the individual churches have roles to play in the quest to spread the good news (#'s 61–62).
3. Individual churches have the task of proclaiming the Gospel in ways that people can understand (#63).
4. Evangelization needs to consider people's concrete lives (#63).
5. While faith may be translated into all expressions, its content must not be impaired (#'s 63–65).
6. There are diverse services in unity in the same mission of evangelization (#66).
7. The Pope has the pre-eminent ministry of teaching the truth (#67).
8. Bishops, priests, religious, laity, young people, and families all have important roles to play in evangelization (#'s 68–72).

10

ON HUMAN WORK

Laborem Exercens, Encyclical of John Paul II, 1981

Major Areas of Concern
—Dignity of Work
—Capitalism and Socialism
—Property
—Unions
—Employment
—Spirituality of Work

On Human Work, Pope John Paul II's encyclical, commemorates the ninetieth anniversary of Pope Leo XIII's *The Condition of Labor*. John Paul II affirms the dignity of work and places work at the center of the social question. The encyclical states that human beings are the proper subject of work. Work expresses and increases human dignity. The Pope stresses the priority of labor over things while criticizing systems which do not embody these principles. He supports the rights of workers and unions. John Paul II concludes by outlining a spirituality of work.

HISTORICAL NOTE

On Human Work represents a clear and succinct statement of John Paul II's thoughts on the social question. Written almost entirely by the Pope himself, the encyclical reflects statements made while he was a Polish prelate and those made during the first years of his pontificate. *On Human Work* develops and refines the Church's teachings on property and its criticism of capitalism and Marxism.

I. Introduction
   1. Humans derive dignity from work even though it involves suffering and toil (#1).
   2. Recent changes in the realm of work (#1):
      a. automation;
      b. increase in price of energy and raw materials;
      c. environmental awareness and respect;
      d. people claiming right to participate.
   3. Role of the Church (#1):
      a. call attention to dignity of workers;
      b. condemn violations of dignity;
      c. guide changes to ensure progress.
   4. Work is at the center of the social question, the key to making life more human (#2).
   5. Catholic social teaching has evolved and now considers the "world" as well as the "class" perspective; the Church calls for structural transformation on a more universal scale (#2).

II. Work and Human Beings
A. Perspective on Work
   1. *Genesis* states God's command to subdue the earth; work is the means to do so (#4).
   2. Human beings are the proper subject of work (#5).
   3. Aspects of technology (#5):
      a. positive: facilitates work;
      b. negative: can supplant or control humans.
   4. Work must serve an individual's humanity (#6).

B. Materialism and Economism
  1. Materialistic thought treats humans as instruments of production rather than as subjects of work (#7).
  2. Workers are considered as merchandise (#7).

C. Justice and Work
  1. Leo XIII's call to solidarity was a reaction against the degradation of people as subjects of work (#8).
  2. Within unemployment of intellectuals, a new "proletarianization" of workers is occurring (#8).
  3. Church is committed to justice for workers; it wants to be a "Church of the poor" (#8).

D. Nature of Work
  1. People achieve dominion over the earth and fulfillment as human beings (#9).
  2. Work and family life (#10):
     a. work makes family life possible;
     b. work makes possible the achievement of purposes of the family;
     c. it increases common good of human family.

III. Conflict Between Labor and Capital
  A. The Conflict
    1. Conflict has changed from one between capital and labor to an ideological struggle and now to a political struggle (#11).
    2. Fundamental principles (#12):
       a. priority of labor over capital;
       b. primacy of people over things.
    3. Humanity has two inheritances: nature, and the resources people have developed (#12).
    4. Need to develop a system that will reconcile capital and labor (#13).
  B. Property
    1. On ownership, Catholic social teaching differs from both Marxism (collectivism) and capitalism (#13).
    2. Right of private property is subordinated to the right of common use (#14).
    3. Property is acquired through work to serve labor (#14).
    4. Socialization of certain means of production cannot be excluded (#14).

5. Church favors a joint-ownership of means of production (#14).

IV. Rights of Workers
Work is an obligation/duty (#16).
A. Indirect Employers
1. Indirect employers (persons, institutions, sets of principles, states, socio-economic systems) determine one or more facets of the labor relationship (#17).
2. Policies need to respect the objective rights of workers—the criterion for shaping the world economy (#17).
B. Employment
1. Suitable employment for all is needed (#18).
2. Indirect employers need to act against unemployment through (#18):
   a. unemployment benefits (springing from principle of common use of goods);
   b. a system of overall planning on economic and cultural levels;
   c. international collaboration to lessen imbalances in the standard of living.
3. Resources must be used to create employment (#18).
C. Workers
1. Just remunerations of workers is the key (#19).
2. Wages are a practical means whereby people can have access to goods intended for the common use (#19).
3. Church calls for (#19):
   a. wages sufficient to support a family;
   b. allowances to mothers raising a family;
   c. reevaluation of the mother's role to ensure proper love for children and fair opportunities for women.
4. Other social benefits for workers are needed, including health care, right to leisure, pension and accident insurance, and a decent work environment (#19).
D. Right to Form Unions
1. Indispensable element of social life (#20).
2. Originated with struggles of workers (#20).
3. Mouthpiece of the struggle for justice (#20).
4. Constructive factor of social order (#20).

5. Can enter political order to secure rights and the common good (#20).
6. Strikes are legitimate but extraordinary (#20).
7. Two cautions (#20):
   a. demands can become "class egoism";
   b. can stray from specific roles.

E. Other

1. Agricultural work is the basis of healthy economies (#21).
2. Disabled people should participate in work (#22).
3. People have a right to leave their native countries in search of better conditions (#23).

F. Elements of a Spirituality of Work

1. Humans share in the activity of their God (#25).
2. Work imitates God's activity and gives dignity (#25).
3. Jesus was a person of work (#26).
4. There are many references to work in the Bible (#26).
5. Vatican II: work allows people to fulfill their total vocation (#26).
6. Work is sharing in the Cross and Resurrection (#27).
7. Work is necessary for earthly progress and the development of the Kingdom (#27).

11

THE SOCIAL CONCERNS OF THE CHURCH

Sollicitudo Rei Socialis, Encyclical Letter of Pope John Paul II, 1988

Major Areas of Concern
—Authentic Development
—North/South Gap
—East/West Blocs
—Solidarity
—Option for the Poor
—Structures of Sin
—Ecological Concerns

Pope John Paul II paints a somber picture of the state of global development in *The Social Concerns of the Church*. He cites the originality of Pope Paul VI's *The Development of Peoples* and emphasizes the moral/ethical dimension of development. After surveying the difficult state of the poor countries, the Pope lays strong blame on the confrontation between the two global blocs, liberal capitalism of the West, and Marxist collectivism of the East. He refers to the obstacles hindering development as the "structures of sin" and calls for conversion toward solidarity and the option for the poor. While he does speak of the responsibilities of the poor countries, by far his strongest challenge is to the affluent world.

HISTORICAL NOTE

Twenty years after *The Development of Peoples*, Pope John Paul II celebrates that encyclical of Paul VI with a strong statement updating the Church's teaching on international development. The document reflects the severity of global economies at the end of the 1980s, with debt, unemployment, and recession seriously affecting the lives of millions not only in the developing countries but also in the more affluent countries. It echoes several of the justice-related themes addressed by the Pope in his worldwide travels.

I. Introduction

    1. Social doctrine seeks to lead people to respond to their vocation as responsible builders of earthly society (#1).

    2. It is marked by continuity and renewal (#3).

    3. Current encyclical celebrates twentieth anniversary of *The Development of Peoples*, and emphasizes need for fuller concept of development (#4).

II. Originality of *The Development of Peoples*

A. Application of Vatican II

    1. It responded to call of *The Church in the Modern World* (#6).

    2. It applied Council's teachings to specific problems of development and underdevelopment (#7).

B. Originality of Message

    1. It emphasized ethical and cultural character of problems connected with development, and the legitimacy and necessity of Church's intervention in this field (#8).

2. It affirmed worldwide dimension of social question, and hence the duty of solidarity between rich and poor (#9).
3. It asserted that "development is the new name for peace," challenging the arms race and linking peace and justice (#10).

III. Survey of Contemporary World

A. Unfulfilled Hopes for Development

1. Twenty years ago there was widespread optimism about possibility of overcoming poverty and promoting development (#12).
2. But in general the present situation is negative (#13):
   a. innumerable multitudes suffer intolerable burden of poverty;
   b. many millions have lost hope, seeing their situation worsened.

B. Widened Gap between North and South

1. Developing countries are falling behind developed in terms of production and distribution of basics (#14).
2. Unity of world is compromised, with division into First, Second, Third, Fourth Worlds (#14).
3. Cultural underdevelopment shown in: illiteracy, lack of participation, exploitation, religious oppression, racial discrimination, etc. (#15).
4. Right of economic initiative, for service of the common good, is often suppressed, frustrating people's creativity (#15).
5. Totalitarianism makes people "objects" (#15).
6. Other forms of poverty exist, e.g., denial of human rights such as right to religious freedom (#15).
7. Causes of worsened situation include (#16):
   a. omissions on part of developing countries;
   b. lack of response by affluent world;
   c. mechanisms (economic, political, social) manipulated to benefit some at the expense of others.
8. Interdependence separated from ethical requirements is disastrous for both rich and poor countries (#17).

C. Specific Signs of Underdevelopment
1. Housing crisis, experienced universally, is due largely to increasing urbanization (#17).
2. Unemployment and underemployment grow, raising serious questions about the type of development pursued (#18).
3. Global debt, forcing debtor nations to export capital, is aggravating underdevelopment (#19).

D. Political Reasons for Underdevelopment
1. Existence of two opposing blocs, East and West, has considerable impact on development of people (#20).
2. Political opposition rests on deeper ideological opposition (#20):
   a. liberal capitalism of the West;
   b. Marxist collectivism of the East.
3. Military opposition results, with tensions of "cold war," "wars by proxy" (#21).
4. Church's social doctrine is critical toward both liberal capitalism and Marxist collectivism (#21).
5. Recently independent countries become involved in, sometimes overwhelmed by, ideological conflict, as two blocs tend toward imperialism, neo-colonialism (#'s 21–22).
6. Exaggerated concern for security blocks cooperation (#22).
   a. Competition between two blocs prevents leadership and solidarity (#23).
   b. West abandons self to growing and selfish isolation (#23).
   c. East ignores duty to alleviate human misery (#23).
7. Arms trade flourishes, refugees are created, and terrorism increases (#24).
8. Demographic problem is often met without respect for persons (#25).

E. Positive Aspects of Contemporary World
1. Awareness grows of dignity and human rights, as expressed in UN's *Declaration of Human Rights* (#26).

2. Conviction increases regarding radical interdependence and solidarity (#26).

3. Peace is seen as indivisible; it is for all, and demands justice (#26).

4. Ecological concern grows, with recognition of limited resources and need to respect nature (#26).

5. Generous persons sacrifice for peace, and international organizations contribute to more effective action (#26).

6. Some Third World countries have reached food self-sufficiency (#26).

IV. Authentic Human Development

A. Challenges to Development

1. Development is not straightforward "progress" in Enlightenment sense (#27).

2. After world wars and with atomic peril, "naive mechanistic optimism" has been replaced by "well-founded anxiety" (#27).

3. Narrow economic emphasis is questioned (#28).

4. Side-by-side with miseries of underdevelopment is inadmissible superdevelopment which involves consumerism and waste (#28).

5. "Having" does not contribute to human perfection unless it contributes to maturing and enriching of "being" (#28).

6. One of the greatest injustices in contemporary world: "poor distribution of the goods and services originally intended for all" (#28).

7. "Having" can detract from "being" if one disregards the quality and ordered hierarchy of the goods one has (#28).

B. Development and Human Nature

1. True development calls for recognition of spiritual, transcendent nature of human beings (#29).

2. Biblical story shows humans developing (#30):

a. having dominion over creation but obedient to Creator;

    b. falling into sin but responding to divine call.

  3. Faith in Christ reveals plan for reconciliation of all to him (#31).

  4. Church therefore has pastoral duty to concern itself with problems of development (#31).

  5. Early teachers of Church had optimistic vision of history and work (#31).

  6. Church cannot ignore needs of the poor in favor of "superfluous church ornaments and costly furnishings for divine worship" (#31).

C. Cooperation for Development

  1. This task is not individualistic; there is an obligation to collaborate with all others in this field (#32).

  2. People and nations have a right to their own development (#32).

  3. Moral character of development requires recognition of rights (#33):

    a. at internal level, respecting life, family, employment, political community, religion;

    b. at international level, respecting peoples, culture, equality of all;

    c. within framework of solidarity and freedom.

D. Respect for Natural World

  1. There is growing awareness of the "cosmos"—the natural order of all beings, living and inanimate (#34).

  2. Natural resources are limited and cannot be used with absolute dominion (#34).

  3. Pollution of the environment threatens the health of all (#34).

V. Theological Reading of Modern Problems

A. Situation of Sin

  1. In years since *The Development of Peoples*, "there has been no development—or very little, irregular, or even contradictory development" (#35).

  2. Main obstacle to development is not political but moral (#35).

3. World divided into blocs, sustained by ideologies, and dominated by imperialism is a world "subject to structures of sin" (#36).
4. Individual actions against neighbor introduce into world influences and obstacles that go beyond individuals, interfering with the development of peoples (#36).
5. Two typical structures of sin are (#37):
   a. all-consuming desire for profit;
   b. thirst for power, imposing one's will on others.

B. Path of Conversion

1. Profound attitudes which define relationships with self, neighbor, and nature must be changed (#38).
2. "Conversion" is needed, toward interdependency, solidarity, commitment to common good (#38).
3. Solidarity requires (#39):
   a. on part of influential, a responsibility and willingness to share;
   b. on part of weaker, an active claiming of rights.
4. Church has evangelical duty to stand by the poor (#39).
5. Solidarity helps us see the "other" as "neighbor," "helper," and is the path to peace and development (#39).
6. As Christian virtue, solidarity is rooted in vision of human beings in relationship to Trinity (#40).

VI. Some Particular Guidelines

A. Church's Social Doctrine

1. Church offers not technical solutions but "set of principles for reflection, criteria for judgment, and directives for action" (#41).
2. It is not a "third way" between liberal capitalism and Marxist collectivism (#42):
   a. not an ideology but a theological interpretation;
   b. a condemnation/proclamation as part of prophetic role.

3. Today especially it must be open to international outlook (#42).

B. Option for the Poor

1. Whole tradition of Church bears witness to "love of preference for the poor," a special form of primacy in exercise of Christian charity (#42).
2. This affects individual action and applies equally to social responsibilities (#42).
3. Growing numbers of poor, in desperate situations, must be a priority in all development plans (#42).
4. The goods of the world are originally meant for all, and hence private property has a "social mortgage" (#42).
5. Special form of poverty includes being deprived of rights, particularly right to religious freedom and right to freedom of economic initiative (#42).

C. Imbalance of International System

1. International trade system discriminates against developing countries, and international division of labor exploits workers for profit (#43).
2. World monetary and financial system compounds poorer countries' problems of balance of payments and debt (#43).
3. Technology transfer is unfair to poorer countries (#43).
4. International organizations need reform, without being manipulated by political rivalries (#43).

D. Responsibilities of Developing Countries

1. Developing countries must take up their own responsibilities (#44).
2. They should promote self-affirmation of their own citizens through programs of literacy and basic education (#44).
3. They need to set priorities (#44):
   a. food production;
   b. reform of political structures;
   c. promotion of human rights.
4. Solidarity among developing countries will call for

greater cooperation and establishment of effective regional organizations (#45).

VII. Conclusion

A. True Liberation

1. There is an intimate connection between liberation and development, overcoming of obstacles to a "more human life" (#46).
2. Church affirms possibility of overcoming of the obstacles, with confidence in the goodness of humans (#47).

B. Urgent Appeal

1. Everyone must be convinced of seriousness of moment and of responsibility to take steps "inspired by solidarity and love of preference for the poor" (#47).
2. As agents of peace and justice, laity have preeminent role in animating temporal realities with Christian commitment (#47).
3. Special cooperation urged with other Christians, with Jews, and with followers of world's great religions (#47).
4. The fact that the Kingdom of God is not identified with any temporal achievement cannot excuse us from lack of concern for concrete situations of today (#48).
5. Eucharist is special call to commitment to development and peace (#48).
6. In Marian Year, we ask Mary's intercession in this difficult moment of the modern world (#49).

12

THE CHALLENGE OF PEACE: GOD'S PROMISE AND OUR RESPONSE

Pastoral Letter of the United States Bishops, 1983

Major Areas of Concern
—Just War
—Non-violence
—Theology of Peace
—Nuclear War
—Deterrence
—Arms Control
—Conflict Resolution
—World Order

The pastoral begins with a preliminary sketch of a theology of peace, building on scriptures and the Catholic just war and non-violent traditions. It moves to a critical discussion of the use of nuclear weapons and the policy of deterrence. The Bishops then propose a number of steps for arms control and conflict resolution. The letter concludes with the Bishops articulating a pastoral response for the Church as it grapples with the issues of war and peace.

HISTORICAL NOTE

The pastoral letter was written by an ad hoc committee of five Bishops chaired by Joseph Cardinal Bernardin. The committee consulted widely among theologians, defense experts, and government officials. The pastoral, heavily influenced by *The Church in the Modern World* and the teachings of Pope John Paul II, went through three drafts before being approved by the National Conference of Catholic Bishops meeting in special session in Chicago in 1983.

Introduction

1. Faith should intensify our desire to tackle the challenges of life (#2).
2. Nuclear war is a more menacing challenge than any the world has ever faced (#3).
3. Letter is invitation and challenge to shape policies in this "moment of supreme crisis" (#4).

I. Religious Perspectives on Peace

1. "The nuclear threat transcends religious, cultural, and national boundaries" (#6).
2. *The Church in the Modern World* provided the Bishops with guidelines for their statements (#7).
3. Different statements in the pastoral carry different levels of authority (#'s 9–11).
4. Three "signs of the times" influence us: world wants peace, arms race is a curse, and new problems call for fresh approach (#13).
5. Two purposes of Catholic teaching on peace and

war: inform consciences and contribute to policy debate (#16).

6. Need for a "theology of peace" which is biblical, pastoral, hopeful (#25).

A. Peace and the Kingdom

1. In the Old Testament:

   a. Metaphor of the warrior God was gradually reformed after the Exile (#31).

   b. Peace is understood in a variety of ways (#32):

      i. is gift of God's saving activity;

      ii. pertains to the unity and harmony of community;

      iii. demands covenantal fidelity of the people to true peace.

   c. Fidelity to God, justice, and peace are all connected (#35).

   d. Messianic time offered hope for the eschatological peace (#36).

2. In the New Testament:

   a. Image of warrior God disappears (#40).

   b. Jesus proclaims God's reign of love and God's gift of peace (#'s 47, 51).

   c. Jesus in his death and resurrection gives God's peace to the world (#54).

B. Kingdom and History

1. Christian view of history is hopeful and calls for a peace based on justice (#56).

2. Bishops are convinced "peace is possible" (#59).

C. Moral Choices for the Kingdom

1. Need to undertake a "completely fresh reappraisal of war" (*Peace on Earth*) (#66).

2. "Peace is both a gift of God and a human work" (#68).

3. In a spirit of love the Christian must defend peace, properly understood, against aggression (#'s 73–78).

4. Just-war criteria attempt to prevent war and limit the conditions that will allow war to happen (#'s 81–84).

   a. *Jus ad Bellum* (why and when war):

      i. just cause—only a real and certain danger (#86);

      ii. competent authority—declared by legitimately responsible public officials (#'s 87–88);

     iii. comparative justice—rights and values involved justify killing (#92);

     iv. right intention—pursuit of peace and reconciliation (#95);

      v. last resort—all peaceful alternatives exhausted (#96);

     vi. probability of success (#98);

    vii. proportionality—damage to be inflicted must be proportionate to the good expected (#99).

  b. *Jus in Bello* (how war is to be conducted):

      i. proportionality—response to the aggression must not exceed the nature of the aggression (#'s 103, 105–106);

     ii. discrimination—not directed against innocent non-combatants (#'s 104, 107).

5. Non-violent commitment:

  a. has rich history in Christian tradition (#'s 111–115);

  b. is not passive about injustice (#116);

  c. includes conscientious and selective conscientious objection (#118);

  d. is stressed as legitimate option for Christian (#119);

  e. is interdependent with just-war teaching in common presumption against force (#120).

II. War and Peace in the Modern World

A. The New Moment

1. Arms race condemned as dangerous, folly, a crime against the poor (#128).

2. "No" to nuclear war must be definitive and decisive (#138).

B. Religious Leadership

1. As moral teachers, we must resist idea of nuclear war as instrument to national policy (#139).

2. We must shape public opinion against rhetoric about winning nuclear war (#140).

C. Use of Nuclear Weapons

1. "Under no circumstances" may nuclear weapons be used against civilian population centers (#147).
2. The initiation of nuclear war is not morally justifiable (#150–153).
3. Bishops are "highly skeptical" about the moral acceptability of a limited nuclear war (#'s 157–161).

D. Deterrence

1. Vatican II and U.S. Catholic Conference statements have weighed deterrence policy benefits (possible prevention of nuclear war) and dangers (escalation of arms race, cost inflicted on poor) (#'s 167–170).
2. Pope John Paul II concludes deterrence may be "morally acceptable" as a step toward progressive disarmament (#173).
3. Deterrence:
   a. is never morally acceptable when it threatens to kill the innocent (#178);
   b. should not result in strategies for fighting wars (#184).
4. The Bishops give a "strictly conditioned moral acceptance" of nuclear deterrence (#186).
   a. No acceptance of "prevailing" in nuclear war (#188).
   b. "Sufficiency" not "superiority" must be goal (#188).
   c. Every new system must be assessed as a step toward "progressive disarmament" (#188).
5. Bishops oppose "first strike" weapons and lowering of nuclear threshold (#190).
6. Bishops recommend bilateral, verifiable "halt" to new systems; bilateral deep cuts in superpower arsenals; comprehensive test ban treaty (#191).
7. Deterrence policy must be scrutinized with greatest care in ongoing public debate on moral grounds (#195).
8. Bishops acknowledge that many strong voices in the Catholic community reject deterrence and call for a

prophetic challenge to take steps for peace (#'s 197–198).

III. The Promotion of Peace

A. Specific Steps

1. The U.S. should take initiative in reduction and disarmament action including:
   a. continual negotiation with potential adversaries (#207);
   b. support for nuclear non-proliferation (#208).
2. The world should:
   a. ban chemical and biological weapons (#210);
   b. control arms exports (#'s 211–213).
3. Conventional forces must also be reduced (#'s 216–218).
4. Civil defense must be examined to see if it is realistic in light of a possible nuclear attack (#220).
5. We must find ways other than force to defend nation's citizens and values (#221).
   a. Non-violent resistance and popular defense need more study (#'s 222–227).
   b. Peace research, conflict resolution studies, peace education programs, U.S. Peace Academy are all endorsed (#'s 228–230).
6. While military service may be required, rights of conscientious and selective conscientious objection must be respected by law (#'s 232–233).

B. Shaping a Peaceful World

1. Peace is not simply absence of war, but presence of justice (#234).
2. Unity of human family and a just world order are central to Catholic social teaching (#'s 235–244).
3. While Americans should have no illusions about the Soviet government, it is in the interest of both superpowers to work for peace, going beyond stereotypes or hardened positions (#'s 245–258).
4. The realization of the world's growing interdependence should lead the U.S. to:

    a. promote structural reform to aid the world's poor (#264);

    b. support reform to make U.N. more effective (#268);

    c. reverse the arms race to make needed resources available for development (#270).

IV. The Pastoral Challenge and Response

A. The Church

1. "To be disciples of Jesus requires that we continually go beyond where we now are" (#276).
2. The Christian must take a stand against much of what the world accepts as right (#277).

B. Pastoral Response

1. Church should develop balanced educational programs about peace, respecting legitimate differences (#'s 280–283).
2. True peace demands a reverence for life, rejection of violence, and an end to abortion (#'s 284–289).
3. Personal and communal prayer is helpful for fostering conversion of hearts (#290).
4. Optional Friday fast and abstinence are tangible signs of penance for peace (#298).

C. Challenge and Hope

1. We must shape climate to make it possible to express sorrow for atomic bombing in 1945 (#302).
2. Many different sectors of American society—including priests and religious, parents and youth, public officials and military personnel—have special requirements to promote peace (#'s 301–327).

Conclusion

1. The Bishops speak as pastors, trying to live up to the call of Jesus to be peacemakers (#331).
2. We need "moral about-face" to say "no" to nuclear war and arms race (#333).
3. The risen Christ helps us confront the challenge of nuclear arms race with trust in God's power (#339).

13

Economic Justice for All: Catholic Social Teaching and the U.S. Economy

Pastoral Letter of the United States Bishops, 1986

Major Areas of Concern
—Biblical Justice
—Option for the Poor
—Participation
—Economic Rights
—Employment
—Poverty
—Agriculture
—Global Economy

Economic Justice for All attempts to apply the major principles of Catholic social teaching to the structure of the U.S. economy.

The Bishops write to provide moral perspective on the economy and to assess the economy's impact on the poor. The Bishops begin their letter with a description of the economy today and develop a moral vision, based on biblical teachings and the tradition of Catholic social thought, of a just economy. They then apply this vision to several policy areas: employment, poverty, agriculture, and international development. They end by calling for cooperation in a "New American Experiment" and a commitment by all sectors of the economy to a future of solidarity.

HISTORICAL NOTE

The U.S. Bishops issued this pastoral letter on the economy in 1986, three and one-half years after their Peace Pastoral. In drafting the letter, the Bishops consulted widely among business leaders, academicians, government officials, and other segments of American society, as well as among theologians and Church leaders. They held several hearings at various locations throughout the United States and received almost twenty thousand written suggestions as they circulated three preliminary drafts. The pastoral is significantly influenced by Vatican II's call to read the "signs of the times," the social teaching of the Council, and the social teachings of Pope John Paul II.

I. The Church and the Future of the U.S. Economy

　　　1. Three questions to shape economic perspective (#1):
　　　　a. What does the economy do *for* people?
　　　　b. What does it do *to* people?
　　　　c. How do people *participate* in it?
　　　2. U.S. economy has many successes but also many failures (#'s 2–3).
A. U.S. Economy Today: Memory and Hope
　　　1. U.S. has high standard of living, productive work, vast natural resources (#6).
　　　2. Economy has involved serious conflict and suffering, and has been built through creative struggle of many (#'s 7–8).
B. Urgent Problems
　　　1. Sign of the times: Preeminent role of U.S. in increasingly interdependent global economy (#10).

2. Mobility of capital and technology affects jobs world-wide (#11).
3. Pollution and depletion of resources threaten environment (#12).
4. Promise of American dream remains unfulfilled for millions in U.S., with high unemployment and harsh poverty (#'s 14–16).
5. Economic life does not support family life (#18).
6. Investment of so many resources into production of weapons increases the problems (#20).
7. Culture/value questions are a deeper challenge to the nation (#21).

C. The Need for Moral Vision

1. Service of the poor: fundamental criterion of economic policy (#24).
2. Pastoral based on Catholic social thought tradition that honors human dignity in community with others and whole of creation (#'s 32–34).
3. Bishops write to (#27):
   a. provide guidance for formation of Catholic consciences;
   b. add voice to public debate on direction of the economy.

II. The Christian Vision of Economic Life

Economic life is to support and serve human dignity (#28).

A. Biblical Perspectives

1. Humans are created in God's image, possess intrinsic dignity, and enjoy gift of creation (#'s 32–34).
2. God's covenant with Israel calls for loving justice which promotes human dignity (#'s 35–40).
3. Jesus proclaims compassion and call to discipleship (#'s 43–47).
4. The preferential option for the poor calls the church "to see things from the side of the poor" (#52).
5. Action for justice proceeds from hope and emphasizes new creation (#'s 54–55).
6. Catholic life and thought about economics are en-

riched through history and learn from other traditions (#'s 56–59).

7. Concerns of letter are central, integral to proclamation of Gospel (#60).

B. Ethical Norms for Economic Life

1. Responsibilities of social living include:
   a. active love of God and neighbor which makes human solidarity and community possible (#'s 64, 66);
   b. establishment of minimum levels of commutative, distributive, and social justice and institutions that support justice (#'s 68–73);
   c. examination of inequalities of income, consumption, privilege, and power (#'s 74–76);
   d. establishment of minimum levels of participation in social institutions (#'s 77–78).

2. Human rights must be respected which:
   a. promote the common good (#79);
   b. include political-civil and social-economic rights as outlined in John XXIII's *Peace on Earth* (#80);
   c. enhance and reflect just institutions (#82);
   d. embody new cultural consensus in U.S. (#'s 83–84).

3. Poor have the single most urgent claim on conscience of nation (#86).

4. U.S. moral priorities should be:
   a. fulfillment of basic needs of the poor (#90);
   b. active participation in economic life by those now excluded (#91);
   c. investment of wealth, talent, and energy for benefit of poor (#92);
   d. strengthening of family life (#93).

C. Working for Greater Justice

1. Through daily work people make their largest contribution to economic justice (#96).

2. Threefold moral significance of work (#97):
   a. principal way for self-expression and creativity;
   b. ordinary way to fulfill material needs;
   c. way to contribute to the larger community.

3. Principle of subsidiarity gives everyone the task of working for justice (#'s 98–99).

4. Workers' right to organize must be respected; just and vital labor unions contribute to the economy's future (#'s 102–109).

5. Business people, managers, owners have a vocation to serve the common good (#'s 110–111).

6. Private property is always at service of common good, and is limited by a "social mortgage" (#'s 114–115).

7. Every citizen has the responsibility to work with others for justice (#120).

8. Government, respecting "subsidiarity," should help groups seeking to promote the common good (#124).

III. Selected Economic Policy Issues

Introduction

1. Church is not bound to any particular economic, political, or social system, but asks: What is impact on people (#130).

2. Our approach is pragmatic and evolutionary, accepting "mixed" economic system and urging its reform to be more just (#131).

3. But larger systemic questions do need to be asked about our economy and its values (#132).

A. Employment

1. Most urgent priority for domestic policy is creation of new jobs with adequate pay and decent working conditions (#136).

2. Unemployment affects eight million people, disproportionately blacks, Hispanics, youth, at severe human costs (#'s 138–142).

3. Current levels of unemployment, assaulting human dignity, are intolerable (#143).

4. Demographic changes, advancing technology, global competition, discrimination, and increased defense spending all have driven up rate of unemployment (#'s 144–149).

5. The U.S. should:
  a. establish consensus that everyone has a right to employment (#153);
  b. coordinate fiscal and monetary policy to achieve full employment (#156);
  c. expand private sector job-training, especially for the long-term unemployed, to establish more socially useful jobs (#'s 156–165);
  d. explore new strategies to improve the quantity and quality of jobs (#'s 167–168).

B. Poverty

1. Poverty, affecting 33 million Americans and dramatically increasing, is "lack of sufficient material resources required for a decent life" (#'s 170–173).
2. Characteristics of today's poverty include:
  a. growing number of children, especially minorities (#'s 176–177);
  b. increasing number of women and female-headed families (#178–180);
  c. disproportionate number of minorities (#'s 181–182).
3. Great inequality in distribution of wealth and income in U.S. affects power and participation and is "unacceptable" (#'s 183–185).
4. Alleviation of poverty in U.S. will require:
  a. fundamental changes in social and economic structures (#187);
  b. programs which empower the poor to help themselves (#188);
  c. doing away with stereotypes that stigmatize the poor (#'s 193–194).
5. Elements of national strategy to deal with poverty include:
  a. sustain an economy that provides just wages for all adults able to work (#'s 196–197);
  b. remove barriers to equal employment for women and minorities (#199);
  c. foster "self-help" programs for the poor (#'s 200–201);

    d. evaluate tax system in terms of impact on the poor (#202);

    e. make a stronger commitment to education for the poor in public and private schools (#'s 203–205);

    f. promote policies which support and strengthen families (#'s 206–209);

    g. reform the welfare system so it respects human dignity (#'s 210–214).

C. Food and Agriculture

1. Increased concentration of land ownership and depletion of natural resources threaten farm life (#217).

2. Structures of U.S. agriculture, affected by new technologies and export orientation, have led to trend of fewer and larger farms (#'s 220–223).

3. Diversity and richness in American society are lost with exodus from rural areas; minorities especially suffer (#'s 225, 229–230).

4. Guidelines for action include:

    a. protect moderate-sized, family-operated farms (#'s 233–235);

    b. safeguard the opportunity to engage in farming (#'s 236–237);

    c. provide stewardship for natural resources (#238).

5. Government should:

    a. assist viable family farms threatened with bankruptcy (#242);

    b. provide more aid to family farms and less to large agricultural conglomerates (#243);

    c. reform tax policies which encourage the growth of large farms (#244);

    d. adopt research, conservation, and worker protection methods (#'s 245–247).

6. Farmworker unions should be supported (#249).

7. Urban and rural cooperation is needed to solve serious agricultural problems (#250).

D. U.S. Economy and Developing Nations

1. In our increasingly interdependent world:

    a. The preferential option for the poor focuses our attention on the Third World (#252).

    b. Developing countries perceive themselves as dependent on industrialized countries, especially the U.S. (#253).

    c. Individual nations, multinational institutions, and transnational corporations are primary actors (#255).

    d. The moral task is to work for a just international order in face of increasing interdependency (#'s 256–257).

2. Catholic social teaching emphasizes love, solidarity, justice, respect for rights, and the special place of the poor as key considerations in forming policy (#258).

3. Fundamental reform in international economic order is called for, with preferential option for the poor the central priority (#'s 259–260).

4. U.S. has central role in building just global economy:

    a. greater support of United Nations (#261);

    b. more attention to human need and less to political strategic concerns (#262);

    c. more cooperation in North-South dialogue (#263).

5. U.S. policy should promote greater social justice in developing world through key policy areas of:

    a. Development assistance: more aid, more multilateral, less military (#'s 265–266);

    b. Trade: fair prices for raw materials and better access for products, while assisting U.S. workers' adjustment needs (#267–270);

    c. Finance: dealing with extremely serious debt problem in ways that do not hurt the poor (#'s 271–277);

    d. Private investment: encourage it while safeguarding against inequitable consequences (#'s 278–280).

6. World food problems offer case of special urgency:

    a. U.S. is in key position and should assist in both long-term and short-term responses (#'s 281–284);

    b. Population policies must be designed as part of overall strategies of integral human development (#'s 285–287).

7. U.S. has a special responsibility to use economic power to serve human dignity and rights, pursuing justice and peace on global scale (#'s 288–292).

IV. A New American Experiment

Preliminary Remarks

1. The founders' attempts to establish justice, the general welfare, and liberty have not been completed (#295).
2. This task calls for new forms of cooperation to create just structures and expand economic participation (#'s 296–297).

A. Cooperation within Firms and Industries

1. Workers and managers need to work together (#299).
2. Profit sharing, worker management, and worker ownership can enhance productivity and justice (#'s 300–301).
3. All sectors should accept a fair share of the sacrifices entailed in making a firm competitive (#303).

B. Local and Regional Cooperation

1. Development of new business is key to revitalizing depressed areas (#309).
2. Entrepreneurs, government, existing business, and the local churches can work together as partners to support revitalization efforts (#'s 309–311).

C. Partnership in Development of National Policies

1. Economy is inescapably social and political in nature (#313).
2. Government and private groups need to work together, planning to form national policy (#'s 314–318).
3. Impact of economic policies on the poor is "the primary criterion for judging their moral value" (#319).
4. Massive defense spending is a "serious distortion" of economic policy (#320).

D. International Cooperation

1. Democracy is closely tied to economic justice (#322).

2. Existing global structures are not adequate for promoting justice (#323).
3. U.S. should support the United Nations in alleviating poverty in developing countries (#324).

V. Commitment to the Future

A. The Christian Vocation in the World
1. Conversion of the heart begins and accompanies structural transformation (#328).
2. Eucharist empowers people to transform society (#330).
3. Laity have the vocation to bring the Gospel to economic affairs (#332).
4. Leisure should be used to build family (#338).

B. Challenges to the Church
1. Church needs to educate the poor and all its members to social justice (#'s 340–343).
2. Economic arrangements must promote the family (#346).
3. Church must be exemplary as economic actor (#347):
   a. pay just wages (#352);
   b. respect the rights of its employees (#353);
   c. make responsible use of its investments and properties (#'s 354–355);
   d. promote work of charity and justice, such as Campaign for Human Development (#'s 356–357);
4. Church commits itself to be model of collaboration and participation (#358).

C. Road Ahead
1. Institutions and ministries of Church will continue to reflect on these important issues (#'s 360–361).
2. Universities and study groups should pursue further research into areas that need continued exploration.

D. Commitment to the Kingdom
1. We must include everyone on the globe in our dream of economic justice (#363).
2. We must move from independence through interdependence to solidarity (#365).

14

TO THE ENDS OF THE EARTH

Pastoral Statement of the United States Bishops, 1986

Major Areas of Concern
—Church as Mission
—Colonialism and Missionaries
—Total Human Liberation
—True Inculturation
—Option for the Poor
—Mission Spirituality

The pastoral states that concern for mission springs from a sense of discipleship. It notes the importance of the local church in mission sending and receiving. The statement articulates a new understanding of Church as mission and stresses that the proper focus of mission is on the physical and spiritual needs of people in the communities. The statement concludes by suggesting a spirituality for missionary activity.

HISTORICAL NOTE

The United States Bishops promulgated this statement to affirm missionaries and to stimulate a sense of personal responsibility in all Catholics for missions. The statement was heavily influenced by Vatican II's *The Missionary Activity of the Church*, Pope Paul VI's *Evangelization in the Modern World*, and Pope John Paul II's *The Apostles to the Slavic People*. In formulating this statement the Bishops relied extensively on principles they first developed in their peace and economic letters.

Introduction

1. Jesus was a missionary (#1).
2. When we promote missionary activity, we are most faithful to the Church (#2).
3. Purpose of statement (#3):
   a. stimulate a sense of personal responsibility;
   b. affirm missionaries.
4. Essential principles for mission are found in *The Missionary Activity of the Church* and *Evangelization in the Modern World* (#4).
5. Concern for mission springs from sense of discipleship articulated in peace and economics pastorals (#6).

I. Missionary Context

A. Historical Background
1. Roots of U.S. Church are in missionary activity (#10).
2. Nineteenth and twentieth centuries: missionaries accompanied immigrants (#11).
3. U.S. Church sent and sends missionaries to other lands (#12).
4. Propagation of Faith and Holy Childhood associations have significantly aided missionaries (#13).

B. Contemporary Developments
1. A new vitality in Latin America, Africa, and Asia (#14).
2. Every local church: mission sending and receiving (#15).

C. A New Self-Understanding
1. Church equals mission (#16).
2. Basic task: spiritual and physical well-being of communities (#17).

3. Colonizing efforts brought strengths and weaknesses of Western civilization (#18).
4. U.S. missionaries: in union with local church, not U.S. government (#19).
5. Missionaries must distinguish their efforts from colonial practices (#20).

II. Today's Task

A. Theological Characteristics
1. Task is rooted in and inspired by Trinity (#22).
2. Mission's urgency springs from Jesus and looks to Kingdom (#'s 23–24).
3. Apostles were foundation of Church and Church continues Jesus' mission (#'s 25–26).
4. Mission: Church's "greatest and holiest duty" (#27).
5. Physical and spiritual needs of others demand response (#28).
6. Dangers from proselytizing are real (#29).
7. Ecumenical efforts: appropriate in prayer, media, social action (#29).

B. Hunger for the Word
1. Spiritual and physical oppression create a hunger for justice and the Word (#30).
2. People: saved as individuals and members of socio-cultural groups (#31).
3. Mission: characterized by respect and concern, not domination (#32).

C. Mutuality in Mission
1. Sharing of the Gospel is essential for local churches (#'s 33, 35).
2. We must be open to the Gospel expressed in a variety of cultures (#36).
3. We need to link Christian values with the good in a culture (#37).
4. Mission is not coercive (#39).

D. Mission and Dialogue
1. Dialogue is necessary for extending Christ's invitation (#40).

2. We must share with the other great religions (#41).
3. Conversion is the goal of missions (#42).
4. Pope John Paul II: Church can offer the "fullness of revealed truth" (#43).
5. True inculturation: Gospel permeates culture (#44).

E. Holistic Approach

1. Gospel demands response to genuine needs (#45).
2. Jesus' mission: liberation (#46).
3. Holy See calls for freedom from cultural, political, economic, and social slavery (#46).
4. Jesus' mission requires our action (#'s 47–48).
5. "The church's mission makes a special option for the poor and powerless" (#49).
6. Evangelization of the powerful is needed (#50).

III. Mission Spirituality

1. Prayerful, Gospel-based spirituality is central to mission (#'s 51, 60).
2. Multiplication of loaves points to sharing (#53).
3. Baptism, Confirmation, and Eucharist nourish mission (#'s 52, 55, 58).
4. Discipleship requires self-denial and gift of life (#'s 56, 59).

Conclusion

1. Young people challenged to become missionaries (#61).
2. Lay missionaries are important (#63).
3. U.S. Catholics have generously supported missionary activity (#'s 64, 66).
4. Education for mission is needed by all Catholics (#70).
5. Gratitude and support for missionaries offered (#'s 72, 73).

15

THE MEDELLÍN CONFERENCE DOCUMENTS

Second Meeting of the Latin American Episcopal Conference, 1968

Major Areas of Concern
—Structural Justice
—Liberation
—Participation
—Marxism and Capitalism
—Political Reform
—Conscientization
—Arms Race
—Violence

The Latin American Bishops—meeting at Medellín, Colombia, in 1968—issued a number of documents on the life of the Latin

American church. The documents on justice and peace (outlined here) apply Catholic social teaching to the Latin American situation. The documents state the need for just structures that promote liberation and participation. Political reform, individual and communal conscientization, and an end to violence are necessary conditions for justice and peace in Latin America.

HISTORICAL NOTE

The second meeting of the Latin American Episcopal Conference—held at Medellín, Colombia, in 1968—coincided with Pope Paul VI's visit to Bogota. Influenced by Vatican II, the social teachings of John XXIII and Paul VI, liberation theology, and the reality of life in Latin America, the Bishops made a seminal and fundamental criticism of society and a strong commitment to the poor.

JUSTICE

I. Pertinent Facts
1. Misery expresses itself as injustice (#1).
2. Recent efforts have not insured justice (#1).
3. Universal frustration of legitimate aspirations exists (#1).
4. Lack of social-cultural integration has caused unjust economic and political structures (#2).

II. Doctrinal Bases
1. God creates people and gives them power to transform and perfect the world (#3).
2. Jesus: liberator from sin, hunger, oppression, misery, ignorance (#3).
3. Authentic liberation requires personal and structural transformation (#3).
4. Divine work equals integral human development and liberation (#4).
5. Love is Christian dynamism (#4).
6. Dignity of human person results in unity of society (#5).
7. Justice: demand of biblical teaching (#5).

III. Projections for Social-Pastoral Planning
A. Direction of Social Change
1. Structures should ensure that all, especially lower classes, participate in society (#7).
2. Families: natural unit of society, should organize so needs can be met (#8).
3. Professional organizations and peasants: organize to demand human and dignified work (#9).
4. Both Marxism and capitalism "militate against the dignity of the human person" (#10).
5. Many workers experience physical, cultural, and spiritual slavery (#11).
6. Participation is necessary for just economic system (#11).
7. Unions "should acquire sufficient strength and power" (#12).
8. Socialization: necessary for unity, liberation, development (#13).
9. Rural transformation needed (#14):
   a. "human promotion of peasants and Indians";
   b. reform of agrarian structures and policies.
10. Industrialization: necessary process for development (#15).

B. Political Reform
1. Purpose of political authority is common good (#16).
2. Political reform needs to address structural change (#16).
3. Political authority: duty to promote participation (#16).

C. Information and Conscientization
1. Formation of social conscience is indispensable (#17).
2. People in decision-making positions deserve special attention (#19).
3. Small, basic communities are essential for this task (#20).
4. Mass media should be used for human promotion (#23).

PEACE

I. Latin American Situation
A. Class Tensions
1. Different forms of marginality: socio-economic, cultural, racial, religious, etc. (#2).
2. Extreme social inequality exists; majority has very little (#3).
3. Inequality breeds frustration and low morale (#4).
4. Privileged are insensitive to misery of marginalized (#5).
5. Dominant class uses power unjustly (#6).
6. The oppressed are increasingly aware of their situation (#7).

B. International Tension
1. Most Latin American countries depend on an external economic power (#8).
2. International commerce is distorted economically (#9).
3. Economic and human capital is invested excessively in foreign countries (#9).
4. A progressive international debt hinders development (#9).
5. International imperialism creates conditions of dependency (#9).

C. Tensions within Latin America
1. Exacerbated nationalism contributes to tensions (#12).
2. The arms race is beyond reason (#13).

II. Doctrinal Reflections
A. Christian View of Peace
1. Peace is a work of justice (#14).
2. Peace is a permanent task (#14).
3. Peace is the result of love (#14).

B. Violence
1. Violence is one of Latin America's greatest problems (#15).

2. Structural justice is a prerequisite for peace (#15).
3. Temptation to violence is strong (#16).
4. Wealthy and fearful must work together for peace (#'s 17–18).
5. People should not put their hopes in violence (#19).

III. Pastoral Conclusions

1. To form the consciences of Latin Americans to peace, justice, and the rights of the poor (#'s 21–22).
2. To encourage Catholic institutions to foster vocations of service (#25).
3. To urge an end to arms race, violence, and domination (#'s 29, 32).

16

THE PUEBLA CONFERENCE DOCUMENT

Third Meeting of the Latin American Episcopal Conference, 1979

Major Areas of Concern
—Evangelization
—Human Dignity
—Liberation
—Base Communities
—Role of the Laity
—Option for the Poor

The Latin American Episcopal Conference—meeting at Puebla, Mexico, in 1979—issued a document that confirmed its statements at Medellín (1968) and placed the entire mission of the Church in the context of evangelization. The document begins by examining the problems confronting the people of Latin America and the role of the Church in solving these problems. The Bishops then consider

God's plan for human beings and the ways that liberation and evangelization can cooperate with this plan. The Bishops next emphasize the roles of base communities and the laity in helping the Church carry out its mission. The Bishops conclude with a strong affirmation of the option for the poor and the option for young people.

HISTORICAL NOTE

The third meeting of the Latin American Bishops, coinciding with Pope John Paul II's journey to Mexico, confirmed Medellín's mandate that the Church evangelize for the poor, for liberation, and for an end to unjust social structures. Although many of the leading progressive Bishops of Latin America were not appointed delegates and most of the region's prominent liberation theologians were not chosen as experts, the conference's final document supported the basic thrust of the social significance of the Church's mission to the world.

I. Pastoral Overview of Latin America

A. Problems
1. Loneliness, family problems, and lack of meaning plague many people (#27).
2. The poverty of millions of peasants, indigenous, and young people is devastating and humiliating (#'s 29, 32–35).
3. Abuse of power has resulted in repression and violation of human rights (#'s 41–42).
4. Materialism has subverted public and private values (#55).
5. Economic, cultural, political, and technological dependence neglects human dignity (#'s 64–66).

B. The Church
1. Present church structures do not meet people's need for the Gospel (#78).
2. Indifferentism, not atheism, is a major problem among intellectuals and professionals (#79).
3. The people are demanding justice, freedom, and respect for rights (#87).

4. Marxism, capitalism, and political activity of priests present dilemmas for the Church (#92).
5. Church supports the people's yearning for a "full and integral liberation" (#141).
6. New social structures and the role of the laity need to be emphasized for Church to fulfill its mission (#'s 152–154).

II. God's Saving Plan

A. Jesus

1. The person of Jesus must not be distorted, factionalized, or ideologized (#178).
2. Jesus "rejects the temptation of political power and the temptation to violence" (#192).
3. Jesus calls for a radical discipleship and a love that give a privileged place to the poor (#'s 192–193).
4. Jesus has planted the Kingdom and justice of God in human history (#197).

B. Human Beings

1. Determinism, psychologism, economism, statism, and scientism offer only partial vision of the human being (#'s 307–315).
2. Church proclaims the "inviolable nobility" and dignity of each human being (#317).
3. Freedom is the gift and task of human beings (#321).
4. Human dignity is rooted in God and renewed in Jesus (#'s 327–330).

C. Evangelization

1. Evangelization "aims at personal conversion and social transformation" (#362).
2. Evangelization seeks to get at the core of a culture to bring about conversion (#388).
3. Urban-industrial culture, accompanied by personalization and socialization, challenges evangelization (#416).
4. Secularism "separates human beings from God" (#435).
5. The people's religiosity is both a way the people

evangelize themselves and an object of evangelization (#450).

D. Liberation

1. Catholic social teaching indicates that the entire Christian community is responsible for evangelization and liberation (#474).
2. Liberation is enacted on the truth about: Jesus, the Church, and human beings (#484).
3. Liberation does not use violence or the dialectics of class struggle (#486).
4. Equality of all peoples, freedom, justice, and self-determination are legitimate aspirations of the people (#'s 502–504).

III. Evangelization

A. Base Communities

1. Base communities foster interrelationships, acceptance of God's word, and reflection on reality and the Gospel (#629).
2. Base communities bring families together in intimate relationships grounded in faith (#641).
3. Base communities embody the Church's preferential love for the common people (#644).

B. Role of the Laity

1. There is a growing need for the presence of lay people in evangelization (#777).
2. An atmosphere of maturity and realism now exists and will promote dialogue and participation in the Church (#781).
3. A clerical mentality and a divorce between faith and life hinder participation in the Church (#'s 783–784).
4. The family, education, social communications, and political activity require the special attention of the laity (#'s 790–791).
5. Lay people need "to acquire a solid overall human formation" to participate more effectively in the mission of the Church (#794).
6. Women have been pushed to the margins of society (#834).

7. Women possess full equality and dignity, and have a significant role to play in the mission of the Church (#'s 841, 845).

IV. A Missionary Church

A. Option for the Poor
1. The poor have been encouraged by the Church (#1137).
2. Jesus' mission is directed to, at first, the poor (#1143).
3. The poor challenge the Church to conversion, service, and solidarity (#1147).
4. Option for the poor requires changes in unjust political, economic, and social structures (#1155).
5. Conversion to evangelize and eliminate poverty demands "an austere lifestyle and a total confidence in the Lord" (#1158).

B. Option for Young People
1. Young people represent "an enormous force for renewal" (#1178).
2. Young people should experience the Church as "a place of communion and participation" (#1184).
3. Church wants to help young people become factors of change (#1187).
4. Church hopes to introduce young people to the living Christ (#1194).

17

JUSTICE AND
EVANGELIZATION IN AFRICA

Statement of the Symposium of Episcopal Conferences of Africa and Madagascar, 1981

Major Areas of Concern
—Christian Vision of Justice
—African Reality
—Church: A Witness for Justice
—Education for Justice
—National and International Action

In 1981 the Bishops of SECAM published an exhortation on *Justice and Evangelization in Africa*. This document states the Christian vision of a just world and contrasts this vision with the situation in Africa. The Bishops issue a call for love and commitment and outline a program of pastoral response for local churches as well as a plan of action on the national and international levels.

HISTORICAL NOTE

This document is the natural cumulation of several SECAM statements on justice, especially denouncements of specific unjust situations. This exhortation is a revision of a Meetings for African Collaboration (MAC) interim report and is the product of extensive consultation between Bishops and other religious leaders.

I. Christian Vision and Today's Reality

A. Christian Vision

1. Jesus came to establish a Kingdom of life, truth, love, and justice (#3).
2. A Church is not fully rooted among its people if it does not try to establish justice (#3).
3. Old Testament (#4):
   a. God's saving justice;
   b. challenge of the prophets to the entire society to be just.
4. New Testament (#5):
   a. Christians should find in the Gospels support for justice activities;
   b. Jesus made himself the champion of the poor, oppressed, marginalized;
   c. call for justice is directed to Jesus.
5. Tradition: justice is an essential basis for Christian life (#'s 5–6).
6. Dedication to the interior virtues of justice and kindness and to the common good is needed to establish a political, social, and economic life that is truly human (#8).

B. Today's Reality in Africa

1. External factors (#'s 9–10):
   a. "liberating" foreign armed intervention creating new states of dependency;
   b. unjust distribution of resources;
   c. dialogue of deaf between North and South;
   d. hold of multinationals;

e. pillage of raw materials from Third World;

f. national debts.

2. Internal factors (#11):

a. violations of human rights;

b. dictatorships, totalitarianism, oppression;

c. corruption of every kind.

C. Call to Love and Commitment

1. Only through love can Christians work in this damaged world (#13).

2. Christians need to work, educate, and commend rather than complain, criticize, and condemn (#13).

II. Pastoral Program for Local Churches

A. Justice in the Church's Life

1. Ongoing conversion in lifestyle and pastoral action (#15).

2. Human relationships of mutual respect (#16).

3. Financial autonomy and sobriety in lifestyle (#17).

4. Respect for cultures (#18).

B. Education for Justice

1. Goals (#20):

a. understand and transmit the good news of human liberation;

b. respect the rights of all.

2. The family: first school of justice; social and cultural changes shake its structures (#21).

3. Youth: justice and service encouraged in formation (#22).

4. Christian communities: responsible for justice in Africa through witness and action (#23).

5. Catholic Action Movements: stress the role of the laity (#24).

6. Communications: great potential for influencing public opinion (#25).

III. National and International Action

A. National Level—Requires the participation of all.

1. Participation in life of society (#27):

    a. application of ethical principles to a society is difficult and delicate;

    b. African tradition emphasizes social responsibility as a duty;

    c. Christians should participate in public life.

2. Identification of the forms of oppression and reflection in common on this oppression, from grassroots up (#28).

3. Joint reflection and action by apostolic workers; "prophets" should speak through the Church (#29).

4. Speaking out for justice (#30):

    a. Jesus loves people and is concerned especially about the poorest and weakest;

    b. prayer for justice is essential;

    c. support of sister-churches is of great help;

    d. action for justice must be action for evangelization;

    e. first priority is to try to dialogue with those responsible for injustices.

5. Structures need to be set up by the Church to document instances of injustices and prepare interventions for justice (#31).

B. International Level

1. Different cultures should be respected (#32).

2. Current international structures operate to detriment of developing countries: e.g., price of raw materials, arms race (#32).

3. Of dramatic urgency is the problem of refugees, the number one plague of African continent (#33).

IV. Conclusion

1. The Spirit will enable people to witness, educate, and work for justice (#34).

2. An appeal is made to churches in the West, to understand and support African Church's efforts (#34).

18

EVANGELIZATION IN MODERN DAY ASIA

First Planning Assembly of the Federation of Asian Bishops' Conferences, 1974

Major Areas of Concern
—Signs of the Times
—Local Church
—Dialogue
—The Poor
—Renewal

The statement by the Federation of Asian Bishops' Conferences emphasizes that the task of evangelization in Asia goes on in a context of profound change and societal transformation. It sees the building up of the local church as the primary focus of evangelization. Central to the mission of the Church is the dialogue with other religions and with the poor. The Bishops see the dialogue with the poor as having consequences for the Church's commitment to justice.

HISTORICAL NOTE

The First Planning Assembly of the FABC met in Taipei, Taiwan, in 1974. It chose as its theme "Evangelization," the same theme as scheduled for the 1974 Synod of Bishops in Rome. The final statement reported the outcome of many workshops at the assembly.

I. Introduction

1. Modern day Asia is undergoing profound change: modernization, secularization, break-up of traditional society, industrialization (#4).
2. We need to read the signs of the times and assist in the promotion of human dignity and freedom (#'s 5-6).

II. Proclamation of the Gospel

In Jesus comes full meaning, liberation, community, peace (#7).

A. Local Church

1. Primary focus of our evangelization is building up a truly local church (#9).
2. It is not an isolated church, but one incarnate with people, indigenous and inculturated (#'s 11-12).
3. It is in dialogue with the great religious traditions of Asian peoples (#'s 13-14).
4. This dialogue enriches our faith understanding, as well as offering to others the way of Jesus (#'s 16-18).

B. Dialogue with the Poor

1. In Asia, dialogue with people means dialogue with the poor (#19).
2. Poor are deprived and live under oppression from

unjust social, economic, and political structures (#19).

3. Dialogue demands (#'s 20–21):
   a. experience of and sharing with the poor;
   b. commitment and effort to bring social justice.
4. Bishops affirm that work for justice is integral to preaching the Gospel and pledge support for those engaged in justice efforts (#'s 22–24).

III. Missionary Formation

A. Elements of Effective Proclamation

1. To preach Gospel is first to communicate experience of the Risen Lord (#30).
2. Contemplative spirit is needed in Asian context (#31).
3. Knowledge of Asian philosophies and ideologies, and understanding of socio-economic factors, are essential in education for mission in Asia (#32).
4. Genuine Asian theological reflection must be given priority (#33).

B. Importance of Mass Media (#34)

IV. Conclusion

1. Message to bearers of Gospel (#'s 35–42).
2. Prayer for blessings (#'s 43–50).

PART THREE

STUDY GUIDE

1

Suggested Uses

WHO?

This book will be useful to many individuals and groups interested in discovering the rich tradition of social teaching in the Roman Catholic Church during recent times:
- —Social Concern Committees exploring the foundations of their task
- —Solidarity organizations and other issue-directed groups researching the Church's tradition of teaching on a particular issue or problem
- —Post-RENEW Groups and adult education programs
- —University and college classes
- —High school "Service" programs
- —Teacher education programs

HOW?

A number of creative uses for this book will undoubtedly arise as groups clarify their own purposes for undertaking a study of Catholic social teaching. Study groups might want to initiate their planning by (1) questioning their own purposes or directions for exploration and (2) choosing a discussion format consistent with their particular needs.

The authors would like to suggest one possible format for the study of these documents. Each study session may consist of three phases:

A. The Descriptive Phase: Discuss the group's understanding of the content of the document in question. Ask:
1. What content seems most familiar in this document?
2. What is new?
3. What is the historical situation to which this text is responding?
4. What, for you, is the most interesting part of the document? Why?

B. The Critical Phase: Relate the document to your own experience. Let the document critique your experience and, in turn, let your experience critique the document. The study questions for each document have been framed to facilitate this process. You might suggest other questions as well.

C. The Action Phase: Explore the action possibilities that the discussion of the document suggests to you and your group, given the particular needs of your community.

A note about the historical study of the documents: The study of documents in the chronological order of their appearance may generate some impatience with material that is dated and less relevant to the contemporary situation. Historical study does, however, have the following advantages: it illustrates the development of concepts, including changes in language and approach; it highlights the historical relativity of the documents (that these are responses to particular sets of circumstances); and it encourages us to be creative rather than imitative in applying the Gospel and the Church's teachings in our own proper situations.

2

Discussion Questions

INTRODUCTION

1. What has been your own experience of the Church's social teachings?
2. What are your feelings about them in general?
3. How important is it for you to have the guidance of the Church's teachings in social matters?
4. Are you or your group searching for social teachings around any particular social issue or problem? Which?
5. Using for reference the document summaries in this book, which documents speak most directly to these issues or problems?

MAJOR LESSONS

1. With which of the twelve major lessons are you most familiar?
2. How did you first encounter these lessons in your education and/or experience?
3. Which other major lessons would you add to the list?

THE CONDITION OF LABOR

1. The working conditions that inspired this document recall images of Charles Dickens's British factories. In your experience, do similar conditions still exist? What principles of this encyclical still apply?
2. What is the condition of workers and their unions in your country? Are their basic rights upheld?

3. How, in your opinion, does the concept of human dignity relate to the rights of the poor community?
4. What is the Church or the government doing to improve the situation of workers and the poor? How can you or your group assist?

THE RECONSTRUCTION OF THE SOCIAL ORDER

1. Some Christians say that the Bishops and the Church have no business meddling in social issues. What is your opinion? How does the Church have a right and a duty to speak on social issues?
2. Discuss the weaknesses of capitalism and socialism as you have experienced them.

CHRISTIANITY AND SOCIAL PROGRESS

1. This document notes the new developments between 1931 and 1961. What, in your view, are the significant developments that have occurred in the world since then?
2. Name three ways in which these new developments affect your life and the life of your community.
3. What would you say is your role as a Christian in the world?

PEACE ON EARTH

1. In 1963, Pope John XXIII listed three significant "signs of the times." Which others would you add to (or subtract from) that list today?
2. For you and your community, what are the three most important rights which Pope John listed?
3. Critique the peace efforts of your community from the perspective of the encyclical.

THE CHURCH IN THE MODERN WORLD

1. What are the most important "joys and hopes, sorrows and anxieties" of our contemporary world? Which ones affect you and your church community the most?
2. Freud referred to religion's function as "illusion"; Marx as

"ideology." In what way would you want religion to function in your community?
3. Should the Church take its agenda from the world? What would this mean in practical ways for the future?
4. List what you believe are the three major things that people need in order to realize their dignity. What factors in your community contribute to or hinder the achievement of this dignity?

THE DEVELOPMENT OF PEOPLES

1. How have you experienced solidarity with people of other nations?
2. In your opinion, how should our nation relate to poorer nations?
3. Efforts at "development" by wealthier nations have not always benefited the poorer nations. What are, from your perspective, the major pitfalls of development efforts?
4. What does the "preferential option for the poor" mean to you?

A CALL TO ACTION

1. Think of one structure in your nation which you would like to change. How can you and the members of your community act to help change this structure?
2. How do you and your church community respond to the challenge of the document to reflect on the contemporary situation, apply Gospel principles, and take political actions when appropriate?

JUSTICE IN THE WORLD

1. Name the major reasons that stimulate you to work for justice. List two factors in your country that foster your work and two factors that hinder it.
2. Discuss how your faith in Jesus helps you to work for justice and peace.

EVANGELIZATION IN THE MODERN WORLD

1. Share with the other members of your group the spiritual journey which has led you to be concerned about justice and peace.

2. This document states that the witness of a truly Christian life is needed for effective evangelization. What impressions do you suppose outsiders have of your local Christian community?

ON HUMAN WORK

1. In what ways does your own work give you a sense of dignity?
2. What aspects of your daily work are dehumanizing? Which are creative?
3. The complexity of today's world scares some people away from social involvement. How do you deal with such complexity?
4. Illustrate, by way of examples from your own work situation, what the "priority of labor over capital" means to you.

THE SOCIAL CONCERNS OF THE CHURCH

1. Why is Pope John Paul II so critical of *both* liberal capitalism and Marxist collectivism? Do you agree that both West and East superpowers share blame for Third World problems?
2. Has the socio-economic life of people in the rich countries improved in the past twenty years? Of people in the poor countries?
3. Why is "development" more than simply economic progress? Is the United States a "developed" country in your opinion?
4. What "structures of sin" could you name in the present global situation?

THE CHALLENGE OF PEACE

1. How is the Old Testament notion of war and peace changed by the life and actions of Jesus?
2. What elements of U.S. defense policy do the Bishops condemn? What elements do they accept? Do you agree?
3. What steps do the Bishops propose that the U.S. take to work actively toward peace?

ECONOMIC JUSTICE FOR ALL

1. How has the U.S. economy helped you and your family to live a more human life? How has the economy hindered your efforts? In what ways do you think the economy helps the poor?

2. What are some of the major principles the Bishops suggest to help us shape a more just economy? List five of the principles which you consider to be the most important.
3. Do you agree with the Bishops when they become very specific in their policy recommendations to meet the economic problems?
4. What are some of the steps which you personally can take to work for a more just economy?

TO THE ENDS OF THE EARTH

1. What are the major elements of the Church's understanding of itself as missionary?
2. What are the principal components of the missionary task today?
3. What can individuals and communities do to involve themselves in the Church's missionary activity?

THE MEDELLÍN CONFERENCE DOCUMENTS

1. What are the ways in which the Bishops ground their recommendations for Latin American society in the Church's social teaching?
2. What aspects of Latin American society do the Bishops think need to be changed? Do you think that this is realistic?
3. In what ways does the injustice in Latin America cause the lack of peace on the continent? What should this mean for U.S. policy in that region?

THE PUEBLA CONFERENCE DOCUMENT

1. What do the Latin American Bishops see as the proper role of the Church in the world? Why do they suggest this role?
2. On what principles does evangelization rest?
3. How are the option for the poor and liberation related to evangelization and base communities?

JUSTICE AND EVANGELIZATION IN AFRICA

1. What factors—internal and external—do you think are most influential in shaping Africa's future?

2. What does it mean to refer to the family as the "first school of justice"? Is this true only in Africa or also elsewhere?

EVANGELIZATION IN MODERN DAY ASIA

1. What is your experience of "local church" as a reality in your area? Is an outreach in evangelization part of your church's mission?
2. If you were to work for greater dialogue with the poor in your area, what would this require? What might be the consequences?

3

BIBLIOGRAPHY

1. Antoncich, Ricardo. *Christians in the Face of Injustice: Toward a Latin American Reading of the Church's Social Teaching.* Maryknoll, NY: Orbis Books, 1987.

> A very perceptive interpretation of the social message from the perspective of the Christian struggle in Latin America; especially helpful in the view of private property.

2. Baum, Gregory. *The Priority of Labor.* New York: Paulist Press, 1982.

> Commentary on John Paul II's *On Human Labor*, with profound explanation of new orientations of Catholic social teaching.

3. Benestad, James, and Butler, Frank (eds.). *A Quest for Justice: A Compendium of Statements of the U.S. Bishops on the Political and Social Order, 1966-1980.* Washington, D.C.: United States Catholic Conference, 1981.

> Complete collection of major statements by U.S. Bishops on a variety of topics.

4. Byers, David M. (ed.). *Justice in the Marketplace: Collected Statements of the Vatican and U.S. Catholic Bishops on Economic Policy, 1891-1984.* Washington, DC: United States Catholic Conference, 1984.

> Collection of primary sources which deal with economic issues.

5. Calvez, J. Y. *The Social Thought of John XXIII.* London: Burns and Oates, 1964.

> Analysis of John XXIII's new approaches to social questions.

6. Calvez, J. Y., and Perrin, J. *The Church and Social Justice: The Social Teaching of the Popes from Leo XIII to Pius XII, 1878-1958.* Chicago: Regnery, 1961.

> Review of major themes of social teaching.

7. Camp, Richard L. *The Papal Ideology of Social Reform: A Study in Historical Development 1878–1967*. Leiden: E.J. Brill, 1969.

> Overview of teaching in historical context of socio-political world.

8. Chenu, M. D. *La "Doctrine Sociale" de L'Eglise comme Ideologie*. Paris: Editions du Cerf, 1979.

> Provocative analysis of the meaning of "social teaching" and its development over the years, with note of the importance of "reading the signs of the times."

9. Cronin, John. *Social Principles and Economic Life*. Milwaukee: Bruce, 1959.

> Readable textbook with applications to concrete situations, but does not treat documents beyond Pius XII.

10. Curran, Charles E., and McCormick, Richard A., S.J. (eds.). *Official Catholic Social Teaching: Readings in Moral Theology, No. 5*. New York: Paulist Press, 1986.

> Excellent collection of essays tracing historical development, issues, and evaluations of the tradition of Catholic social teaching.

11. Desrochers, John. *The Social Teaching of the Church*. Bangalore, India: John Desrochers, 1982.

> Historical analysis of development of major teachings of both Catholic and Protestant churches.

12. Dorr, Donal. *Option for the Poor: A Hundred Years of Vatican Social Teaching*. Maryknoll, NY: Orbis Books, 1983.

> Helpful analysis of each of the major papal and conciliar documents.

13. Eagleson, John, and Scharper, Philip (eds.). *Puebla and Beyond*. Trans. John Drury. Maryknoll, NY: Orbis Books, 1979.

> Complete texts from 1979 Puebla Conference of Latin American Bishops, plus very insightful commentaries.

14. Gibbons, William J., S.J. *Seven Great Encyclicals*. New York: Paulist Press, 1963.

> Contains the texts of *The Condition of Labor* and *The Reconstruction of the Social Order*.

15. Gremillion, Joseph (ed.). *The Gospel of Peace and Justice: Catholic Social Teaching since Pope John*. Maryknoll, NY: Orbis Books, 1975.

> Collection of major documents of 1961–1974, with excellent introductory essay on themes and detailed index.

16. Mainelli, Vincent P. *Social Justice: The Catholic Position*. Washington, DC: Consortium Press, 1975.

> Documents from 1961–1974, with helpful index to major themes.

17. Masse, Benjamin L., S.J. *Justice for All: An Introduction to the Social Teaching of the Catholic Church*. Milwaukee: Bruce Publishing Company, 1964.

Textbook of major economic themes up through John XXIII.

18. Mueller, Franz H. *The Church and the Social Question*. Washington, DC: American Enterprise Institute, 1984.

Reprint of historical essay on the influences on social teaching up to early 1960s.

19. Novak, Michael. *Freedom with Justice: Catholic Social Thought and Liberal Institutions*. San Francisco: Harper and Row, 1984.

Critical review of the socially progressive trends in the Church's teaching by a prominent neo-conservative.

20. O'Brien, David, and Shannon, Thomas (eds.). *Renewing the Earth*. New York: Doubleday Image, 1977.

Collection of major documents including important U.S. statements.

21. Second General Conference of Latin American Bishops. *The Church in the Present-Day Transformation of Latin America in the Light of the Council*. Two volumes. Washington, DC: United States Catholic Conference, 1973.

Contains position papers and conclusions from 1968 Medellín Conference.

22. Walsh, Michael and Davies, Brian (eds.). *Proclaiming Justice and Peace: Documents from John XXIII to John Paul II*. Mystic, CT: Twenty-Third Publications, 1984.

Contains key social documents of the past two decades.

A NOTE ON AVAILABILITY OF DOCUMENTS

The documents outlined and discussed in chapters 1 to 10 of this book can be found in a number of widely available sources, including some of those listed above. The documents discussed in chapters 11 to 18 can be obtained in the following ways: for copies of John Paul II's *Sollicitudo Rei Socialis* and the U.S. bishops' pastoral letters on peace, the economy, and mission, contact the United States Catholic Conference, Publications Office, 1312 Massachusetts Ave., NW, Washington, DC 20005-4105; for the documents from the Latin American bishops, see numbers 13 and 21 in the bibliography, above; for copies of *Justice and Evangelization in Africa,* contact the Symposium of Episcopal Conferences of Africa and Madagascar (SECAM), 4 Senchi Street, P.O. Box 9156, Airport, Accra, Ghana; for copies of *Evangelization in Modern Day Asia,* contact the Federation of Asian Bishops' Conferences, P.O. Box 2984, Hong Kong.

About the CENTER OF CONCERN

The Center of Concern is an independent, interdisciplinary team engaged in social analysis, theological reflection, policy advocacy, and public education on issues of peace and justice. Rooted in a faith commitment and guided by a global vision, our current programs focus on international development, peace initiatives, economic alternatives, women in society and church, the cultural crisis, and social theology. The Center holds consultative status with the United Nations. Our team engages in an extensive program of workshops and writing to help North Americans understand and respond to the changing global scene. A newsletter, *CENTER FOCUS,* is published bi-monthly. The Center is a tax exempt group and is supported largely by donations from friends.

CENTER OF CONCERN
3700 13th Street, N.E.
Washington, D.C. 20017
(202) 635-2757